Understanding
ERICH MARIA REMARQUE

UNDERSTANDING MODERN EUROPEAN and LATIN AMERICAN LITERATURE

JAMES HARDIN, *Series Editor*

ADVISORY BOARD

Understanding Günter Grass
by Alan Frank Keele

Understanding Graciliano Ramos
by Celso Lemos de Oliveira

Understanding Gabriel García Márquez
by Kathleen McNerney

Understanding Claude Simon
by Ralph Sarkonak

Understanding Mario Vargas Llosa
by Sara Castro-Klarén

Understanding Samuel Beckett
by Alan Astro

Understanding Jean-Paul Sartre
by Philip R. Wood

Understanding Albert Camus
by David R. Ellison

Understanding Max Frisch
by Wulf Koepke

Understanding Erich Maria Remarque
by Hans Wagener

Understanding Elias Canetti
by Richard H. Lawson

Understanding Thomas Bernhard
by Stephen D. Dowden

Understanding Heinrich Böll
by Robert C. Conard

UNDERSTANDING

ERICH MARIA
REMARQUE

HANS WAGENER

UNIVERSITY OF SOUTH CAROLINA PRESS

Copyright © 1991 University of South Carolina

Published in Columbia, South Carolina, by the
University of South Carolina Press

Manufactured in the United States of America

Library of Congress Cataloging-in-Publication Data

Wagener, Hans, 1940–
    Understanding Erich Maria Remarque / Hans Wagener.
      p.   cm. — (Understanding modern European and Latin American
  literature)
    Includes bibliographical references (p.   ) and index.
    ISBN 0-87249-740-2 (hard cover : acid-free)
    1. Remarque, Erich Maria, 1898–1970—Criticism and interpretation.
I. Title. II. Series.
PT2635.E68Z94   1991
833'.912—dc20   91-6890

CONTENTS

EDITOR'S PREFACE

Understanding Modern European and Latin American Literature has been planned as a series of guides for undergraduate and graduate students and nonacademic readers. Like its companion series, *Understanding Contemporary American Literature*, the aim of the books is to provide an introduction to the life and writings of prominent modern authors and to explicate their most important works.

Modern literature makes special demands, and this is particularly true of foreign literature, in which the reader must contend not only with unfamiliar, often arcane artistic conventions and philosophical concepts, but also with the handicap of reading the literature in translation. It is a truism that the nuances of one language can be rendered in another only imperfectly (and this problem is especially acute in fiction), but the fact that the works of European and Latin American writers are situated in a historical and cultural setting quite different from our own can be as great a hindrance to the understanding of these works as the linguistic barrier. For this reason, the UMELL series will emphasize the sociological and historical background of the writers treated. The peculiar philosophical and cultural traditions of a given culture may be particularly important for an understanding of certain authors, and these will be taken up in the introductory chapter and also in the discussion of those works to which this information is relevant. Beyond this, the books will treat the specifically literary aspects of the author under discussion and attempt to explain the complexities of contemporary literature lucidly. The books are conceived as introductions to the authors covered, not as comprehensive analyses. Nor do they provide detailed summaries of plot since they are meant to be used in conjunction with the books they treat, not as a substitute for the study of the original works. The purpose of the books is to provide information and judicious literary assessment of the major works in the most compact, readable form. It is our hope that the UMELL series will help to increase our knowledge and understanding of the European and Latin American cultures and will serve to make the literature of those cultures more accessible.

Professor Wagener's *Understanding Erich Maria Remarque* is a fascinating study of a soldier turned writer whose life incredibly spanned the chasm from trench warfare to Hollywood. Considering the enormous commercial success that Remarque's novels have enjoyed over the past sixty years—Remarque is quite probably the most widely read German author in the English-speaking world—there is remarkably little solid criticism about his work in its entirety. Wagener traces the career of a man whose life and writings all too faithfully mirror the horrifying events of the twentieth century: World War I, the inflation, the crash, the rise of Hitler, the exile of German intellectuals, World War II, and the Holocaust. And one of the primary strengths of the present work is that it shows thematic links among the many novels of Remarque in a way that has not been done up to now, and which provides insights into the oeuvre as a whole. The book will especially interest readers who know *All Quiet on the Western Front* but who have not read the later novels, some of which reveal the suppressed passion of that greatest of all war novels.

ABBREVIATIONS

Book titles cited in the text are abbreviated as shown below. The page numbers following these abbreviations refer to the original American editions listed in the Bibliography.

AQ = *All Quiet on the Western Front*
AT = *Arch of Triumph*
BO = *The Black Obelisk*
F = *Flotsam*
HF = *Heaven Has No Favorites*
NL = *The Night in Lisbon*
RB = *The Road Back*
SL = *Spark of Life*
SP = *Shadows in Paradise*
TC = *Three Comrades*
TL = *A Time to Love and a Time to Die*

CHRONOLOGY

June 22, 1898   Erich Paul Remark was born in Osnabrück; the son of bookbinder Peter Franz and Anna Maria Stallknecht Remark.

1904–12   Attended Catholic elementary schools in Osnabrück.

1912   (Easter) Entered the *Katholische Präparande* in order to prepare for the profession of elementary school teacher.

1916   Entered the Catholic Teachers College.

Nov. 21, 1916   Drafted from school into the army. Basic training at the Caprivi-Kaserne and later in a camp at Celle.

June 12, 1917   Sent to the western front.

July 31, 1917   Wounded by shell fragments from English artillery; taken to the St. Vincenz hospital in Duisburg; released on October 31, 1918.

Jan. 1919–Aug. 1, 1919   Completed teacher training program at the Teachers College in Osnabrück.

Aug. 1, 1919–Nov. 20, 1920   Various assignments as a substitute teacher in nearby villages.

1920   First novel, *Die Traumbude* (The Dream Room), published by Verlag der Schönheit in Dresden.

1921–22   Various jobs, including salesman for the Vogt Brothers' stone-cutting and gravestone firm in Osnabrück, and Sunday organist in the chapel of a mental hospital.

Oct. 1922   Moved to Hannover and worked as editor and publicity director for the Continental Rubber Company. Editor of *Echo Continental,* the company's advertising and trade journal.

Jan. 1925   Moved to Berlin; *Sport im Bild* picture editor.

Oct. 14, 1925   Married Jutta Ilse (Jeanne) Zambona.

1927–28   *Station am Horizont* (Station on the Horizon) serialized in *Sport im Bild.*

Nov. 10–Dec. 9, 1928   *All Quiet on the Western Front* serialized in *Die Vossische Zeitung.*

Jan. 31, 1929   *Im Westen nichts Neues* (*All Quiet on the Western Front*) appeared in book form.

Jan. 4, 1930   Divorced from Jeanne Zambona.

April 30, 1931 *Der Weg zurück* (*The Road Back*) published in Germany and the United States.

1931 Bought a villa on Lago Maggiore (Porto Ronco) in Switzerland.

Jan. 29, 1933 Left Germany to live in Switzerland.

April 26, 1937 *Drei Kameraden* (*Three Comrades*) published in America; German edition in Amsterdam in 1938.

Jan. 22, 1938 Remarried Jeanne Zambona in St. Moritz, Switzerland.

July 4, 1938 Loss of German citizenship.

March 23, 1939 Arrival in New York from Le Havre on the *Queen Mary*. Back to Europe in June 1939. Back to New York on the *Queen Mary*, September 4, 1939.

April 1941 *Liebe deinen Nächsten* (*Flotsam*) published in America; German edition in Sweden the same year.

1946 *Arc de Triomphe* (*Arch of Triumph*)

Aug. 1947 U.S. citizenship acquired in New York.

1948 Returned to Switzerland to live there.

1952 *Der Funke Leben* (*Spark of Life*).

June 1954 *Zeit zu leben und Zeit zu sterben* (*A Time to Love and a Time to Die*) published in America; German edition the same year.

1956 *Der schwarze Obelisk* (*The Black Obelisk*).

Sept. 20, 1956 Premiere of *Die letzte Station* (*The Last Station*) in Berlin.

May 20, 1957 Second divorce from Jeanne Zambona.

Feb. 25, 1958 Married actress Paulette Goddard in Branford, Connecticut.

1961 *Der Himmel kennt keine Günstlinge* (*Heaven Has No Favorites*).

1962 German edition of *Die Nacht von Lissabon* (*The Night in Lisbon*); American edition 1961.

Sept. 25, 1970 Died in Saint Agnese hospital in Locarno, Switzerland.

1971 German edition of *Schatten im Paradies* (*Shadows in Paradise*); American edition 1972.

Oct. 5, 1973 *Full Circle,* an adaptation of *The Last Station* by Peter Stone, premiered in Washington, DC.

Oct. 5, 1988 Premiere of "Die Heimkehr des Enoch J. Jones" (The Homecoming of Enoch J. Jones) in Osnabrück.

Understanding
ERICH MARIA REMARQUE

INTRODUCTION

W hen we think about certain periods of history, epoch-making books come to mind that capture the spirit of those times most vividly. They determine in large part the way we see these times today and the way we feel about them. That is not to say that what we read is necessarily an objective account or that under close scrutiny we can even term it realistic. However, such books communicate not only information but also the feelings and the sufferings of a people of a particular time. One such book is Erich Maria Remarque's *All Quiet on the Western Front* (*Im Western nichts Neues*; 1929), an enormously popular novel about World War I that was translated into many languages and gave to millions of people the perspective of the common soldier in the trenches. The gripping story of the sufferings and deaths of the protagonist, Paul Bäumer, and his small group of friends was interpreted worldwide as a manifesto for pacifism and antimilitarism. An American film based on the book, released in 1930, reinforced this interpretation. All of these—book, film, and the author himself—became the subject of heated political debate in Germany at a time when Hitler's Nazi party was on the rise. In retrospect, one might think that Remarque's advocacy of peace and humanity—and his statements against militarism—might have been in vain. But they were not invalidated by the Third Reich, and remain in the minds of his millions of readers all over the world.

Following the publication of the novel, Nazi propaganda tried, in its typically crude way, to smear Remarque's name by claiming that he was a French Jew, that his real name was Kramer, which he had reversed and expressed the "k" by writing it as "que," according to French orthography. The actual fact is that the object of Nazi vilification was born Erich Paul Remark on June 22, 1898, in the Westphalian town of Osnabrück, the third of four children of Peter Franz Remark and his wife, Anna Maria (Stallknecht).[1] An older brother died in childhood in 1901. Thus Erich Paul grew up with his two sisters, Erna and Elfriede. All were baptized in the parents' Roman Catholic faith. The Remark family had immigrated from France several generations previously, and when Erich Remark changed his last name to Remarque in 1923, he unwittingly restored the original spell-

1

ing. At that time he also replaced the common middle name Paul by the more poetic Maria, probably modeled after the poet Rainer Maria Rilke.

The author grew up in lower-middle-class, almost poverty-level conditions. The father, a bookbinder by trade, was a serious man without a sense of humor. He moved his family often in order to save money by paying lower rent, sometimes within one single street in the same town. Remarque was not very close to him, while he felt very close to his mother, who would suffer from cancer and would have to be operated on repeatedly.

Erich Paul Remark was a bright, perceptive student who had a strong interest in music, art, and literature. Since he was musically talented, he received instruction in piano, and later he even played the organ. In 1915 and 1916 he supplemented his meager pocket money by giving piano lessons to young people. For a while he seriously considered a career as a pianist. According to his own later statements he was prevented from realizing his musical career because of a shrapnel wound above his right wrist received during World War I. His boyhood hobbies were fishing in a local canal as well as butterfly and stamp collecting. After attending elementary school he entered the Catholic *Präparande* (preparatory school) in 1912 in order to prepare for admission to the Catholic Teachers College to which he transferred in 1916. Becoming a teacher was one of the few options open to him as the son of parents with a modest financial background, the other being to become a minister. Thus, apart from the fact that this offered Remarque the possibility to further his education, he resigned himself to becoming an elementary school teacher because of the job security and limited prestige such a position held and, above all, to please his mother, who wanted to see her son in a secure position for the rest of his life. Pursuing his artistic and especially his literary interests, he joined a group of like-minded youths under the leadership of the somewhat older Osnabrück poet and painter Fritz Hörstemeier. The youth group, consisting of aspiring painters, musicians, and artists, met in Hörstemeier's attic apartment and discussed literature and the arts as viewed from their free, vitalistic philosophy.

Before he could complete his teacher's training, Remarque was drafted on November 21, 1916, together with his classmates. After a short military training at the Caprivi-Kaserne (Caprivi barracks) a few miles northwest of Osnabrück and at Celle in Lower Saxony, he was sent to the western front, to Flanders, where he served in a sapper unit whose task it was to fortify positions behind the front by laying barbed wire and building gun emplacements, bunkers, and dugouts, all within range of enemy gunfire. On

July 31, 1917, he was wounded by fragments from English long-range artillery shells and transported to an army hospital in Duisburg. His wounds were in the neck, the left leg above the knee, and the right forearm.

While he was still in the hospital, on September 9, 1917, Remarque's mother died from cancer. Erich received leave to attend her funeral. Later news reached him about the untimely death—he was just thirty-six years old—of his friend and mentor Fritz Hörstemeier on March 6, 1918. Remarque was as deeply affected by his friend's death as if a member of his family had died. He again received leave to attend the funeral in Osnabrück and played the organ for the service. During his hospital stay Remarque continued his interest in writing. He submitted a sketch entitled "Aus der Jugendzeit" (From the Time of Youth), a short story, "Die Frau mit den goldenen Augen" (The Lady with the Golden Eyes), a poem, "Ich und Du" (Me and You), to the Dresden periodical *Die Schönheit,* all extremely romantic pieces which were published in 1918.

After his final release from the hospital on October 31, 1918, Remarque was first declared fit for garrison duty and sent to Osnabrück. On November 7 the batallion physician declared him fit for field duty; he was going to be sent back to the front, but the war ended within a few days (November 11, 1918).

During the following months Remarque was seen several times wearing war decorations he was not entitled to, and during the following year he was even seen in Hannover wearing a lieutenant's uniform as well as a monocle.[2] In January 1919 he returned to Osnabrück to finish his education, which he completed during the summer of the same year. He subsequently held several substitute teaching positions in villages not far from Osnabrück, but they were not to his liking. His request to be released from any further teaching assignments was granted on December 12, 1920. As Harley Taylor points out, "Remarque's rejection of teaching as a profession had been decided by him even before his abortive career began. He never really wanted to be a teacher and made the choice originally only because he wanted to please his parents and because nothing better offered itself."[3]

In the meantime Remarque had published several more pieces in *Die Schönheit.* His first novel, *Die Traumbude* (The Dream Room), which he had been working on since 1918, was published during the same year, 1920, by the Verlag der Schönheit. In order to subsidize the printing costs Remarque had to pawn his piano. The novel is a roman à clef for which Remarque's own circle of friends around Fritz Hörstemeier provided the models. In *Die Traumbude* Hörstemeier appears under the name of

Schramm, supervising the personal life and careers of his young disciples. Ernst Winter, a young music student and a composer, obviously representing Remarque himself, shares Schramm's living quarters with the "dream room" where the circle of friends meet. The meager plot of the novel revolves around Ernst, who is torn between the honest Elisabeth and a cunning femme fatale named Lanna Reiner, an opera singer whom he courts in Leipzig. After Schramm dies, Ernst comes home and is united with Elisabeth. The impressionistic, romantic tale in which a number of Remarque's poems are interspersed shows the author as a young Romantic who feels drawn to the arts and who wants to break out of the narrow-mindedness of his bourgeois hometown environment.

During the following years Remarque continued trying his hand as a freelance writer and submitted many poems and various articles to newspapers such as the *Osnabrücker Landeszeitung* and to magazines. At the same time he held all kinds of odd jobs, working as a clerk, an accountant, a salesman for the local gravestone company owned by the Vogt Brothers; in 1921–22 he played the organ on Sundays for religious services in a state mental hospital. In October 1922 he left Osnabrück to become editor for *Echo Continental,* a magazine published by the Continental Rubber Company in Hannover, and publicity manager for the company. He wrote verses praising the merits of Continental automobile and bicycle tires as well as other rubber products (inflatable rubber boats, water hoses, tennis balls, coats, bathing caps); cartoon strips depicting adventures of the Contibuben (Continental rascals), patterned after Wilhelm Busch's Max and Moritz characters; and others featuring a certain Captain Hein Priemke.

Apart from the cultural and social attractions of the city of Hannover, which was far less provincial than Remarque's native Osnabrück, his job offered him the opportunity for extensive travel to European car races, other sporting events, and resorts. Thus, while working for Continental, he traveled in Italy, France, Switzerland, the Balkans, and Turkey. In January 1925 he moved to Berlin and began working as picture editor for the Scherl Publishing House's weekly magazine *Sport im Bild* (Sport in Picture), which gave Remarque the opportunity to continue his contacts with sports personalities. Remarque was now in the vibrant German capital with its cafés and boulevards, its nightlife, its theaters, and its many other artistic and sports events. That he made every effort to become part of this new world is evidenced by the fact that with the first sizable amount of money he was able to save, 500 marks, he had himself adopted by an impoverished nobleman, a certain Freiherr (Baron) von Buchwald, so that from now on

Remarque could add the insignia of nobility to his calling cards. As late as 1929 he was still registered as Erich Freiherr von Buchwald, gen. (called) Remark. After the success of *All Quiet on the Western Front* he no longer considered it necessary to use the questionable title of nobility in order to impress people.

On October 14, 1925, he married his former colleague from Continental, the attractive Jutta Ilse (Jeanne) Zambona, who had come to Berlin with him from Hannover. This first marriage ended in divorce in 1930, although during the following two years the couple went out together to social events and to the theater, and they traveled together.

Remarque's literary effort during these years included an essay published in *Sport im Bild* in 1927 entitled "Hymne auf den Cocktail" (Hymn to the Cocktail) and a novel about car racing, *Station am Horizont* (Station on the Horizon), which was serialized in *Sport im Bild* late in 1927 and in the first issues of 1928. Following the tremendous success of *All Quiet on the Western Front* in early 1929, Remarque quit his job with *Sport im Bild*.

Suddenly rich and famous, he enjoyed the good life, buying in 1931 a villa in Porto Ronco on Lake Maggiore in Switzerland, where he consequently took up residence. Hated by the Nazis because of the pacifistic nature of *All Quiet on the Western Front*, he narrowly escaped imprisonment when they came to power in January 1933. Just having returned to Germany from Switzerland, he almost accidentally left again, thus escaping certain persecution. He described his departure in an interview with Robert van Gelder on January 27, 1946. Van Gelder reports:

> Remarque's agent found him one morning at about four o'clock and urged him to go to Switzerland and start work on a new book that he had contracted to write. "There was fantastic luck again," said Remarque. "I considered, should I order another drink and then go home to bed, or should I order another drink, get into my car and drive to Switzerland. I decided it would be better if I woke in Switzerland the next day and started work at once than if I slept in Germany and drove to Switzerland the next day. That is why I was in Switzerland when the Nazis came to hunt for me." The Nazis would have better served themselves Remarque says, had they followed him into Switzerland and killed him.[4]

His works were among those publicly burned in Berlin in front of the Opera House on May 11, 1933. Students and Nazi speakers announced and denounced the authors whose books were thrown into the fire. When it was

Remarque's turn, the speaker shouted: "Against literary betrayal of the soldiers of the World War, for the education of the nation in the spirit of truthfulness. I consign to the flames the works of Erich Maria Remarque."[5]

There is little doubt that Remarque could have avoided the public burning of his books and subsequent exile if he had given in to the wooing by the Nazis. Joseph Goebbels, the propaganda minister of the Third Reich, had extended to him the offer to leave him and his books untouched if he would attribute all responsibility for the film *All Quiet on the Western Front* to his "Jewish" publisher, Ullstein. Although Remarque in fact had nothing to do with the film, it testifies to his personal integrity that he did not accept the offer.

Like many of Germany's foremost writers, Remarque now was in exile. Until the outbreak of World War II in September 1939 he was free to travel in Europe outside Switzerland, except to Germany. He thus drove in his Lancia—which he loved to drive at high speeds—to places such as Davos, St. Moritz, Venice, Rome, Paris, and the French Riviera, frequenting expensive restaurants and nightclubs in the company of beautiful women, including the German actress Marlene Dietrich. He developed a particular liking for Paris, which became almost his second home during these years.

Remarque married Jeanne Zambona a second time in St. Moritz, Switzerland, on January 22, 1938, enabling her to remain in Switzerland and later to emigrate to the United States. This second marriage was dissolved on May 20, 1957, in Juarez, Mexico. The Nazis took away Remarque's German citizenship on July 4, 1938, and after a first visit to the United States in March 1939, he finally left Europe in September 1939 with a Panamanian passport on the last peacetime voyage of the *Queen Mary*. He lived in Los Angeles until 1942, when he moved to New York, which because of its urbanity was more to his liking. In the above-quoted interview with Robert van Gelder he expressed his frustrations about Los Angeles:

> There always was someone in the bar, but the streets out there are deserted. No one walks. You know, that's ugly. In the country I take it for granted that I won't meet anyone, but there are animals, the life of the country. But to walk in a city where there are rows upon rows of buildings and sidewalks extending for miles and people nowhere to be seen, only buildings and automobiles—ah, ghastly. Hollywood is ghastly anyway. I had nothing to do with pictures, never went near a studio [which is simply an error], but the ghastliness of it crept into me and I had to come away.[6]

In New York, Remarque soon became a regular guest at fancy restaurants and nightclubs such as 21 and Stork Club. As late as 1957 he said in an interview with *Newsweek:*

> I now think of New York as my home. It is an unbelievable city. There is virtually everything here. I am very happy to have become an American. I have met exceedingly cultivated people in America. Americans have an innate sense of freedom, whether they realize it or not. They act toward each other that way. It is so easy to mix with others. This freedom is something it is very hard for a European, who has not observed it, to conceive of.[7]

Because of the success of his books and their film versions in the United States, Remarque was spared the poverty and professional frustrations of many other German exile writers. But the Nazis took revenge on their un-favored writer by murdering his sister Elfriede. She was accused of defeat-ist remarks and beheaded with an ax on December 16, 1943. Roland Freisler, the infamous judge of the People's Court who was presiding over her trial, specifically told her that "because her brother was beyond the control of the court she would have to atone for his guilt."[8]

During his exile years in America, Remarque enjoyed the friendship of such celebrities as Marlene Dietrich—their affair lasted, with interrup-tions, approximately until 1942—, Greta Garbo, Ingrid Bergman, the Ger-man writer Lion Feuchtwanger, and Alma Mahler-Werfel, then the wife of the Austrian exile writer Franz Werfel. His social life suffered considerably from the curfew which was imposed on all "enemy aliens," restricting Re-marque to his home from 6 P.M. until 6 A.M. each day. During his stay in Los Angeles he first lived in a bungalow of the fashionable Beverly Hills Hotel, and then he rented a house at 1050 Hilts Avenue in Westwood. In New York he first occupied a corner suite in the Ambassador Hotel on Park Avenue; in the summer of 1953 he rented an apartment at 320 East 57th Street. Remarque did not become an American citizen until 1947. He re-turned to Europe in 1948 to live in Porto Ronco, and occasionally moved back to New York for short intervals. After 1966 he usually spent the winter months in Rome. On February 25, 1958, Remarque married the film star Paulette Goddard with whom he had been close friends since 1953, at a quiet wedding ceremony in Branford, Connecticut. Just as Remarque had been married before and had had close relationships with a number of fe-male celebrities, Paulette Goddard had been married before to Edgar James, Charles Chaplin, and Burgess Meredith. This marriage was going to last, however, until Remarque's death on September 25, 1970, in a hospital in Locarno, Switzerland.

There is no doubt that Remarque's books always dealt—either directly or indirectly—with subject matter that he knew from personal experience or that had at least been triggered by events affecting him personally. To completely understand his novels, we must therefore examine the autobiographical background and the personal references alluded to in the text. Remarque's life and his novels are closely related, and through his protagonists he tries to impart a humanitarian message to his reader.

In his novels Remarque covered all important periods of German history experienced during his lifetime. However, his novels do not relate events in the manner of a historical novel where concrete events and the characterization of a period of history are of primary importance. Instead, he always focuses on how history plays with the individual and his aspirations. The individual is depicted as one threatened by history, endangered, who tries to escape the effects of history, be it war, the aftermath of war and poverty, or persecution due to race or political conviction. Remarque deals in this way with World War I, the Weimar Republic, and the Third Reich. The Third Reich he describes in two respects: first, World War II and the events and atmosphere inside the Third Reich, including the concentration camps; second, the plight of the exiles who had to flee from the Third Reich as Jews or as political activists. Moreover, if we discount his posthumously produced play, "The Homecoming of Enoch J. Jones", and his novel *Heaven Has No Favorites* (*Der Himmel kennt keine Günstlinge;* 1961), which contains few references to the postwar period, Remarque did not deal with post-1945 events in any of his works, except in terms of mere warnings appended to or contained in several of his later novels.

NOTES

1. The most detailed account of Remarque's life is found in Harley U. Taylor, Jr., *Erich Maria Remarque: A Literary and Film Biography.* (New York: Peter Lang, 1989). Much biographical detail is also to be found in C. R. Owen, *Erich Maria Remarque: A Critical Bio-Bibliography* (Amsterdam: Rodopi, 1984).

2. Taylor 25; Owen 13–14.

3. Taylor 36.

4. Robert van Gelder, *Writers and Writing* (New York: Scribner's, 1946) 380–81.

5. Quoted by Joseph Wulf, *Literatur und Dichtung im Dritten Reich: Eine Dokumentation* (Gütersloh: Sigbert Mohn, 1964) 45.

6. van Gelder 379.

7. *Newsweek* Apr. 1, 1957: 108.

8. Taylor 167.

CHAPTER ONE

All Quiet on the Western Front
(*Im Westen nichts Neues*)

In 1928 Remarque felt depressed in his situation as the editor of *Sport im Bild*. As he stated in an interview, he realized that the reason for this depression and feeling of desperation was his war experience, and he observed similar feelings in his friends and acquaintances.[1] He thus sat down and wrote *All Quiet on the Western Front* as a therapeutic attempt to rid himself of these feelings. He began writing after returning home from his office one evening, and finished the book within a period of six weeks.

It is difficult to summarize the plot of *All Quiet on the Western Front* in terms of one logical story line, since Remarque intends to describe neither a linearly developing action nor a psychological development. He wishes instead to characterize the condition of being at war. He also describes the state of being estranged from everything that one's former life and home represented. Consequently this novel consists of a number of short episodes that describe typical war experiences such as food disbursements, artillery barrages, gas attacks, furloughs, watch guards, patrols, visits to a comrade in the army hospital, rats, latrines, and so on. The story is told in the first person except for the final paragraph, where an anonymous narrator is introduced who reports Paul Bäumer's death. The novel in its original version is only 288 pages long and consists of twelve relatively short chapters, each containing several episodes.

Influenced by their patriotic teacher Kantorek, who during drill time gave the class long lectures, asking the young students in a moving voice: "Won't you join up, Comrades?" (AQ 9), the young Paul Bäumer and his classmates volunteer to join the army during World War I. Their military boot camp training, headed by the vicious sergeant Himmelstoss, is a rude awakening. They are soon sent to the front, where they experience the gruesome reality of a war in the trenches with several somewhat older soldiers, including Bäumer's mentor Katczinsky (Kat). When Bäumer returns home during leave, he is unable to identify with the memories of his youth. Nor can he understand the patriotic enthusiasm of the older generation, including his father who wants proudly to show off his son as a hero. Consequently he is happy to go back to this comrades where he feels he belongs. During a patrol Bäumer stabs a Frenchmen who jumps into the same shell crater where he is hiding, and he witnesses the Frenchman's slow, painful death. Later he is himself wounded and experiences the horrors of war in an army hospital. Back at the front, he sees his comrades die one by one, until he too is finally killed.

In *All Quiet on the Western Front* Remarque deals with the last two years of World War I from the perspective of the common soldier in the trenches. Although it is not a historical novel, does not mention battles by name or give their exact dates or geographical places, a knowledge of the political background of World War I and the postwar years is nevertheless essential for understanding the novel and its reception in Germany.

Germany had gone to war in 1914 on the side of Austria against Russia in the east and against France and England in the west. Germany's hope for a quick victory in France by marching through Belgium, thus violating its neutrality, had crumbled as early as 1914. The unsuccessful attacks of German volunteers in Flanders, particularly at Langemarck in the fall of 1914, had claimed many lives and brought the German advance to a halt. The war in the trenches had begun. Large offensives mounted in the following years had failed—the Germans could not break through the French lines, nor could the French and British troops break through the German lines. 1916 marked the year of two great battles—the Verdun offensive and the battle of the Somme. Both battles resulted in hundreds of thousands of casualties on both sides. In the latter battle, for instance, some fifty thousand English troops were killed or wounded in the first three days of battle. As a result, the German armies were severely depleted and ever younger recruits were drafted. Due to a British blockade the German people were starving. In order to break the blockade Germany escalated its submarine warfare. This in turn led, after the sinking of the *Lusitania,* which carried some American passengers but also war munitions, to the United States' intervention on April 2, 1917, on the side of the Allied Powers. From that point on, Germany had to fight against not only armies with superior manpower, including the fresh American troops that arrived in Europe, but also against an overwhelming advantage in the quantity and quality of war materials, medical and food supplies. An armistice between Germany/Austria and Russia was declared after the czar and his government were toppled in the 1917 Russian Revolution. This event ultimately resulted in the separate Peace of Brest-Litowsk (March 3, 1918).

The military relief gained from this peace at the eastern front came too late for Germany. Several German offensives in 1918 were to a large extent unsuccessful because temporary gains could not be exploited due to lack of reserves. Tanks, used by the Allied Powers since November 1917, were a modern weapon rare in the German army. After several successful French offensives the German front gave way. Germany had gone on the defensive, and it became clear that Germany could not win the war. Negotiations for an armistice resulted in the Allied insistence on terms Germany considered insulting, and as a result the German fleet was ordered to resume fighting. This order provoked a sailors' revolt on October 28, 1918, which quickly spread all over Germany. Workers' and soldiers' councils were elected locally and took power. The Bavarian king was forced to flee; Emperor William II abdicated and went into exile in the Netherlands. On November 11, 1918, an armistice was concluded and the Peace of Versailles was signed on June 18, 1919.

This summarizes the historical framework of *All Quiet on the Western Front*. However, Remarque rarely mentions any specific historical facts or geographical locations, thus making it easy for millions of readers to identify with the characters of the novel. At the same time, Remarque's vagueness makes it impossible to localize the events in any specific time or place. Remarque recounts only subjective individual experience, that is, those experiences that are generally excluded from official historiographies. Only in the second half of the novel does he allude to the fact that the war is coming to an end, and he specifically mentions that Bäumer "fell in October 1918" (AQ 291), so that we roughly know that we are dealing with 1917–18.

Remarque prefaces his book with the following:

This book is to be neither an accusation nor a confession, and least of all an adventure, for death is not an adventure to those who stand face to face with it. It will try simply to tell of a generation of men who, even though they may have escaped its shells, were destroyed by the war.

This statement is a key to understanding the author's intention in writing his book and to the novel's "message." Since the book is not intended to be an accusation, the author clearly states that he did not consciously wish to make any political statement, not even one advocating pacifism. The phrase "simply to tell" implies on the one hand that the book is going to relate mere facts. On the other hand, however, this phrase denies the wish to "confess." This denial can also be interpreted as Remarque's own denial that this novel is an exact autobiographical account of his war experiences.

Although written as a first-person narrative, the book is a fictional work and not an autobiography. Paul Bäumer should not be confused with Remarque. Indeed, Remarque has stated in an interview that he himself experienced most of the things he is reporting here, but it is also true that many things he just heard from others, especially from his time in the Duisburg hospital, and through letters from his friends. Working as a sapper, Remarque was in an area that was exposed to enemy shelling—otherwise he could not have been wounded. However, we must not forget that he did not actually serve on the front line, nor did he ever participate in hand-to-hand combat or direct attacks and counterattacks. Thus, Remarque himself had experienced the war only from the perspective of a sapper and as a patient in an army hospital. Many other aspects of the book are in fact autobiographical, particularly the scenes about boot camp in the barracks, the camp on the moors, furlough, work as a sapper, getting wounded, and being in the army hospital. However, these autobiographical elements are carefully interwoven into a work of fiction. It is unfair to take the author to task for having deviated from his own biography, as many of his contemporary critics have done.

The second aspect of the statement that prefaces the novel is that he is reporting about a generation of men who were destroyed by the war even though they escaped its shells. What he is thus saying is that his report has a general application and validity; that he wants to report not about an individual but about a collective fate. Furthermore, he implies that he does not want to tell us about the war experiences of young people, at least not solely, but rather wishes to justify the inability of young people to successfully cope with life after war, that is, life during the Weimar Republic. Such an interpretation focuses not on the war itself but on the year 1928, the very year when Remarque was writing his novel. One may very well argue that he uses his war experience to justify his own lack of professional success after the war, his inability to choose a solid career, and particularly his initial lack of success as a writer immediately following the war years.[2] There is no doubt that the notion of an entire generation ruined by war and unable to function contributed decisively to the book's success. Many readers were readily able to identify with the novel's heroes and found a ready-made justification for their own inability to cope with life during the Weimar years. The "lost generation" theme, coined by American writer Gertrude Stein, also plays an important role in the work of Ernest Hemingway, as can be seen in the epigraph for *The Sun Also Rises* (1928).

A third theme of the novel is also alluded to; namely, that of survival in war. Remarque claims that any war survival will at best be a physical survival and can never be an emotional or psychological one.

In his very first chapter Remarque jumps into the war action: "We were at rest five miles behind the front" (AQ 3), he states. Throughout the novel it is not always apparent from the immediate context whether "we" refers to the entire military unit or only to the narrator, Paul Bäumer, and his immediate group of friends—here the latter is more probable. His immediate friends include his former classmates from high school, Albert Kropp, Müller, and Leer, as well as some more mature friends—Tjaden, a locksmith; Haie Westhus, a peat cutter; Detering, a farmer; and the forty-year-old Stanislaus Katczinsky, called Kat. Remarque does not present these soldiers as complete, psychologically developed characters. In fact, each is merely characterized as having universal human qualities that appear as leitmotifs in the text: Tjaden is the biggest eater of the company; Kat has a sixth sense for danger, good food, and soft jobs; Haie Westhus continually has women on his mind; and Detering longs for his farm. Thus, these soldiers actually can be placed into two distinct groups: the former students and the somewhat older generation who had already had a job and usually a wife. When Remarque refers to the lost generation, he does not mean the older comrades who were already rooted in a profession or family of their own, but the students whose youth was cut short and ruined by the war. These students never had a career or wife, and have nothing to come back to after the war, nothing that would provide a secure place for them in society. Later, the term "generation" also applies to a broader group of all young people whose life was ruined by the war.

The group of friends presented by no means includes representatives of the entire society. Workers and representatives of the upper strata of society are missing. Sociologically speaking, the friends thus represent a homogenous group of members of the lower middle class, the class to which Remarque himself belonged.

In chapter 1, only 80 out of 150 men in the "Second Company" return back to the camp from the front lines. The remaining 80 soldiers are happy to receive food for 150 men. "Stomach" and "digestion" are repeatedly mentioned and become the two most important themes for the soldiers. One scene—left out of the earlier American editions—describes a soldier sitting in a latrine for two hours. This event is described as a recreational idyll where soldiers can talk and rest.

13

In a flashback Kantorek, the class's former teacher, is introduced. Kantorek had so indoctrinated the boys with his patriotic speeches that the entire class consequently volunteered to join the army. (Remarque himself was drafted and had not volunteered.) For Remarque, Kantorek is a representative of the thousands of well-meaning but misguided teachers in pre-World War I Germany who sent young men into the war while themselves staying home. In Remarque's opinion this is a clear indication of the shortcomings of the older generation. Educators who were supposed to guide the younger generation into the world of adulthood, into the world of work, duty, culture, and progress, have failed. The youth's belief that their elders have greater insight and wisdom was shattered by their sight of the first war casualties. All that these teachers had taught them—their entire world—view crumbled during the first artillery barrage. Remarque stresses the fact that these young soldiers were not cowards. They are described as courageously advancing in each attack. They love their country, but have begun to see how they have been betrayed. They now see the old world as a façade, that their education had no practical application. They are not provided with the necessary spiritual, intellectual, and psychological tools to deal with the experience of war. Remarque's statements resound as a reproach to the older generation. It is important to note that Remarque also underscores the conservative virtues of soldierly courage and love for one's homeland. This resulted in some initial positive reviews of *All Quiet on the Western Front* in right-wing newspapers and magazines.

The small group of former students visit their former classmate Kemmerich in the field hospital. He has had one leg amputated and is dying. Müller is interested in a pair of soft leather British pilot's boots that Kemmerich will never be able to wear again. Kemmerich first refuses, but during a second visit, described in chapter 2, he asks the narrator to take the boots along for Müller. Already before the second visit the narrator interjects an extensive passage pointing out that simply because Müller wants to have Kemmerich's boots does not mean that he has less compassion for him than someone who does not dare think of it. If the boots would be of any use to Kemmerich, Müller would do anything to get hold of them for Kemmerich, but it is clear that Kemmerich will die soon. At the front line only the facts count. In this way Remarque demonstrates how conventional modes of behavior and thinking have been turned upside down by the war. Being a soldier means to forget about conventional emotions and behavior. These must be superseded by a pragmatic analysis of the situation at hand. The boots themselves also have symbolic significance. Müller, who now has the boots, is killed. They are then passed on to Tjaden, and after Tjaden is killed, to the narrator, Paul Bäumer, thus foreshadowing his death.

At the end of chapter 1 the narrator laments the loss of his youth: "Youth! We are none of us more than twenty years old. But young? Youth? That is long ago. We are old folk" (AQ 17). The war has aged them before their time; it has deprived them of their youth.

The motif reappears at the beginning of chapter 2. The narrator points out that these soldiers have been cut off from their youth by underscoring the difference between the former students and the older soldiers. Because of their interests, professions, and families of their own, these older soldiers are more firmly rooted in their former lives and are able to return to and continue their lives. For them the war is just an interruption of their activities during times of peace. The students, on the other hand, do not know what the future will hold for them. A touch of pathos and sentimentality marks this section of the novel, a trait that unfortunately became much more pronounced in several of Remarque's later works.

After the scene with Kemmerich's boots, the narrator recalls the time when he and his classmates volunteered for the army full of idealized and romantic feelings about the war. He then bemoans their tough boot camp training, which required the denial of all idealistic values of their former education. However, he also admits that giving up their individual personalities was necessary to survive. The narrator thus indirectly supports the necessity of carrying out seemingly sadistic behavior in a wartime situation. After describing in detail the deliberate harassment by Sergeant Himmelstoss, he concludes: "We became hard, suspicious, pitiless, vicious, tough—and that was good; for these attributes had been entirely lacking in us. Had we gone into the trenches without this period of training most of us would certainly have gone mad. Only thus were we prepared for what awaited us" (AQ 25). The sergeant's dehumanizing and depersonalizing viciousness may be described as a necessary element of survival in war, but the statement made remains an indirect comment on the nature of war itself.

The friends do not break apart; they "adapt," and a feeling of togetherness awakes in them. Remarque feels that this comradeship is the only positive thing that the war has produced. It is again something found in many war novels or, to be precise, in many novels about the front lines written by politically right-wing authors. However, closer analysis reveals that this comradeship also includes a readiness to help one's fellow comrade. This readiness to help, however, is deeply rooted in the will to survive, which is only possible with the reciprocated help of the other comrade.

After Kemmerich dies and Paul Bäumer leaves the hospital, a great, joyful feeling at simply being alive fills him. A feeling of lust for life overcomes him, and he seems to be getting this inner strength from the earth through the soles of his shoes: "The earth is streaming with forces which pour into me through the soles of my feet. . . . My limbs move supple, I feel my joints strong, I breathe the air deeply" (AQ 32). Remarque often uses such contrasts; and here when describing this rapturous state, this frenzy of life that seizes the narrator, he describes a kind of biological vitalism typical of his time. This kind of life-cult permeates all of his work from the first to the very last.

In chapter 3 ever younger recruits are brought in to replenish the company and fill in the gaps created by the mounting number of casualties. The detested Himmelstoss comes to the front, and Paul Bäumer's friends take their revenge by beating him up one night. Marxist critics have often interpreted this as Remarque's own private revenge on the older generation.[3] Many of Remarque's statements about war support this claim. Here in chapter 3 Kropp suggests that wars really ought to be fought by the state secretaries and generals dressed in swim trunks and armed only with sticks. Clearly Remarque is not a political person. There are no detailed plans for organized resistance, nor does he advocate a utopian socialist state.

The tendency to mythologize is also apparent in chapter 4, where the group is brought to the front to dig new trenches. The noises heard from the front awaken the soldiers' senses, electrifying them, and making them more alert. The front has an incredible power of attraction. The earth is envisioned as the protective force which gives the soldier shelter, taking him in and protecting him. The influence of the front forces the soldiers to regress by many thousands of years. They become animals with bestial instincts that are the sole means for survival. This too is testimony to the dehumanizing effect of war. However, it also becomes clear in the following that even Remarque is not insensitive to an aesthetic appreciation of war, as he describes the shining backs of the horses in the moonlight, the beauty of their movements, and the sparkling of their eyes. The horsemen with their steel helmets look to the narrator like knights from a time long past, a scene that appears somehow beautiful and touching to him:

> The backs of the horses shine in the moonlight, their movements are beautiful, they toss their heads, and their eyes gleam. The guns and the wagons float before the dim background of the moonlit landscape, the riders in their steel helmets resemble knights of a forgotten time; it is strangely beautiful and arresting (AQ 56–57).

Such passages are not very different from right-wing war novels. Such heroic descriptions of war are reminiscent of the German writer Ernst Jünger, who considered war a steel bath, a storm of steel that tests character and forges a new man.

Suddenly a massive artillery barrage not only scares the young recruits but also kills and injures many "screaming" horses in a horrifying scene. At the end of the episode the farmer Detering asks a rhetorical question about the horses' guilt and considers it the most horrible aspect of war that innocent animals are involved. This argument is designed to make the reader question the soldiers' own guilt and the reasons they "deserve" to be in the war. After another surprise attack, including a gas attack, the same argumentation is transferred to the young recruits and at the end Kat shakes his head saying: "Young innocents———" (AQ 73).

In chapter 5, after discussing the news that Himmelstoss has been sent to the front line, the friends discuss life after the war. Although Haie Westhus first thinks about catching up on his sex life, he would ultimately like to stay in the army. The life of a sergeant seems more attractive to him than the hard life of a poor peat cutter. Army life in times of peace is described in almost idyllic terms. Tjaden insults Himmelstoss verbally, which results in several days' confinement for him. In this scene Remarque demonstrates that the rules governing the front line are very different from those governing the camp. In one conversation the friends mock the lessons they were taught in school, assignments that have no practical application in war. Connections to cultural values and traditions have disintegrated. They can no longer communicate with those who stayed at home, and the continuity of development from their childhood to their current stage in life has been lost. These former students do not know how they can possibly continue when the war is over. After their experience it is inconceivable to them that they could get accustomed to a professional career. This inability to imagine any meaningful future after the bigger-than-life experience of war is seen by Remarque as the experience of an entire generation represented by Paul Bäumer and his friends. They have been spoiled by war, he maintains, spoiled for everything in life. They have nothing to believe in any more except war, and they feel lost. This is the main theme of the novel. It clarifies the perspective from which it is written, although its logic is not completely consistent. Neither Paul Bäumer nor any of his friends have been psychologically shattered by the war. They are now able to see all the patriotic phrases of their teachers in perspective, and they realize that their book knowledge has no apparent application. However, they are not broken;

they do not get the opportunity to prove that they are part of the lost generation because they are killed one by one. Instead, Remarque demonstrates a kind of quiet heroism, a heroism that was created perhaps for the wrong reasons. But it is nevertheless a kind of heroism through which these young men are proving themselves.

Although Remarque condemns Himmelstoss and his methods of preparing the recruits for war, he also points out the usefulness of his hard, repetitious drills. The company leader, Lieutenant Bertinck, is presented as a reasonable human being ("He is a decent fellow" [AQ 91]) who gives Tjaden only the minimum punishment for insubordination. "They used to tie us to a tree," Remarque comments, "but that is forbidden now. In many ways we are treated quite like men" (AQ 91). This is perhaps one of the strongest indictments of the spirit of Prussian militarism. Here it is not the war that makes the soldiers regress by thousands of years, turning them into animals, but the militaristic spirit of those who do not consider soldiers human beings.

It is interesting to see that every time he describes an intense war scene, Remarque interjects scenes of soldiers resting in the camp, thus skillfully interspersing his novel with action and rest. In this case he even paints an idyllic picture of the soldiers in a manner reminiscent of picaresque novels. The soldiers are described stealing and frying a goose, eating it in a deserted shack, and sitting together surrounded by death. The final words of the chapter describe an emotional celebration of comradeship: "but by my side, stooping and angular, goes Kat, my comrade" (AQ 97).

In chapter 6 the sight of coffins piled high announces a new offensive. Paul Bäumer philosophizes about the importance of coincidence as the sole reason for a soldier to survive. Such arguments, of course, nullify much of the rightist notions of manhood and bravery. If a soldier stays alive in a modern war only as the result of a coincidence, all personal bravery and heroism is for naught in the battle for survival. Remarque goes on to describe the effects of continued heavy artillery barrages, the crumbling trenches, young recruits going berserk, and the sequence of attack and counterattack. He describes how the soldiers turn into animals without personal enemies. It is death itself that they fight against full of rage. Fighting is not done out of patriotism or heroism, but purely out of a feeling of instinctive survival:

We have become wild beasts. We do not fight, we defend ourselves against annihilation. It is not against men that we fling our bombs, what

18

do we know of men in this moment when Death with hands and helmets is hunting us down. . . . We feel a mad anger. No longer do we lie help-less, waiting on the scaffold, we can destroy and kill, to save ourselves, to save ourselves and be revenged (AQ 113).

In sharp contrast to this desperate description is an idyllic vision of the hometown, as idealized by childhood memories. Remarque describes an al-ley of poplar trees and a brook which he recalls from his own town, Osna-brück. These poplar trees and the brook often appear in his novels. They signify the innocence and peace of a lost youth. Remarque again laments the impossibility to connect with the past after the experiencing of war and concludes: "I believe we are lost" (AQ 123). Thus, the soldiers' situation is described as a life with no link to the innocence of youth. Their ability to conform to a regular, bourgeois life after the war has been destroyed by the war as well.

The fighting continues. It is disheartening to see the ill-trained recruits get wounded and killed because of their lack of experience. The lamenta-tion about the lost youth is transferred directly to the front line in this pas-sage by describing how the youth is now killed before the eyes of the "lost generation." In the course of these war activities Haie Westhus is killed. The mention of the trees changing color marks the passage of time: It is fall now, no year is given. This time the company of 150 has been reduced to a total of 32, thus indicating the severity of the losses in this advanced stage of the war.

Chapter 7 finds the rest of the company in the camp again. Food and rest are the two basic needs of a soldier. He can bear the horrors of war only when he does not think about them. And it is this condition of not thinking that also prevents reflection about the causes of war. Humor and obsceni-ties, one might add, are weapons for survival. Remarque postpones the great discussions and arguments about the fundamental issues until after the war. To be sure, his remarks have a threatening tone, but he is so unclear, so uncertain about what he says, that his words admit his (or rather Paul Bäumer's) inability to clearly visualize the coming revolution, as he con-cludes this pensive interjection by declaring: "We shall have a purpose, and so we shall march, our dead comrades beside us, the years at the Front behind us:—against whom, against whom?" (AQ 141).

Remarque provides variety in this otherwise unrelievedly grim story by introducing women. First he describes friends discussing a poster with a picture of a pretty, clean girl which is in stark contrast to the soldiers' dirty condition. The poster depicts a kind of utopian dream. Consequently they decide to get rid of their lice. But reality is different from the pictured dream. They cross a canal and meet for several nights with some French girls who feel sorry for the German boys and make love with them in return for army bread. This is an attempt to try to forget the reality of war, although Paul Bäumer comments that "a man dreams of a miracle and wakes up to loaves of bread" (AQ 154). In war, Remarque is bitterly saying, even love is reduced to pragmatism. Love is something that belongs to the private sphere. Thus the uniforms and boots, the symbols of anything soldierly and thus also the war, must remain outside when they enter the French girls' house.

Then Bäumer is given seventeen days' leave, including three days for travel, and he uses them to return home. Many aspects of this visit home are clearly autobiographical. The town described resembles Remarque's hometown, Osnabrück. A glass box with butterflies Bäumer had collected as a boy hangs on the wall—just as in Remarque's own home. Bäumer has a close relationship with his mother in the text, while that to his father is more distanced, just like Remarque's own. Moreover, his father is identified as a bookbinder by trade and his mother is described as seriously ill, dying of cancer, just as in Remarque's case. During his military training Remarque himself received time off to visit his sick mother.

Bäumer's furlough is marked by unhappy personal experiences. When he fails to see an old major on the street, he is forced to go back and salute him according to military etiquette. Remarque tells his reader that at home the old traditions are still—for now—strictly adhered to, whereas the realities of war force different rules at the front. For a front-line soldier such formalities are petty harassment. The reality of the front and the dream world of those who have stayed at home are contrasted time and again. For Bäumer it is already an embarrassment that his father would prefer him to wear a uniform so that he could proudly present his heroic son to his acquaintances. For Bäumer such a demonstration would constitute a misrepresentation of the reality of war. His father would like him to relate his front-line experiences. Bäumer considers it dangerous to put his experiences into words for fear that they will take on a kind of reality with which he would be unable to cope. At this point, as elsewhere in the novel, he is afraid to acknowledge what is happening "out there" at the front. The experience of realization is simply too frightening and would itself threaten his life since it would take away from the act of mere survival.

His father also takes him aside and leads him to a table in the inn reserved for regular guests. Here the old generation still clings to patriotic phrases and unrealistic territorial claims in a war they expect Germany to win. The contrast between the military stalemate and the reality of dying at the front, on the one hand, and the official patriotic optimism of 1914 which has been preserved at home, on the other hand, once again becomes clear.

Bäumer must realize that he has changed under the impact of the war experience and that the world at home—once so familiar—now alienates him. It is this feeling of strangeness, a feeling of not belonging, an inability to connect with the past, be it with his mother's naïve concerns or the schoolboy's world, that prevails in this entire important episode. This feeling is most clearly symbolized by the old books Bäumer peruses on his bookshelf. These books represent the lost youth he mourns, the old quiet passions and wishes, the impatience of the future, and the lofty joy of the world of thought. They describe the spiritual and intellectual world which he has created for himself outside of school. However, the books are unable to bring back his youth or to melt the heavy, dead block of lead which has formed deep inside him. It is here that Bäumer realizes that his youth is past, that memories have been reduced to shadows, and that the presence of war has erased all that he considered beautiful.

Remarque has presented this experience of estrangement and loss with a certain quiet pathos and sentimentality. We must ask ourselves whether it is justified to blame this supposed loss of youth only on the war and whether the realization of these hard realities is not something every young person has to endure at the end of his teen-age life. Rather than allowing the individual to develop in the process of growing up, to allow him to slowly become conscious of the new reality of adulthood and the impossibility of realizing the dreams of puberty, the war accomplishes this through a kind of shock therapy. The maturing process is shown as a necessary development that everyone must go through, one that war does not allow.

A lighthearted picaresque interlude follows this reflective scene, as is often the case in the novel. While visiting his old classmate Mittelstaedt in the local army barracks, Bäumer sees at first hand how his old patriotic teacher Kantorek is being drilled for active duty. A friend of Bäumer's, also a former student, takes revenge on the teacher for former humiliations in the classroom. But serious overtones appear as well. Kantorek had coerced a student by the name of Joseph Behm to volunteer and this boy was consequently killed three months before he would have been drafted. Thus Remarque underscores the guilt of the older generation symbolized by the patriotic teacher Kantorek. Bäumer visits Behm's mother, assuring her that her son was indeed killed instantly, and when she insists, Bäumer even swears an oath that he died without suffering. Bäumer maintains that he himself would not come back from war if it were not true, which clearly foreshadows his ultimate death.

Before Bäumer goes back to the front, he must attend a military training course in the camp on the moors. Remarque interrupts the novel here with this chapter in order to present a new, more human picture of the enemy. Here it is the Russian prisoners of war who are housed in an adjacent camp with very little to eat. Remarque characterizes them positively by describing them as having the faces of "meek, scolded St. Bernard dogs" (AQ 191) or as having good farmers' faces. This description also implies that they should be threshing, reaping, and picking apples. In other words, by making these people soldiers, Remarque not only describes them as having been estranged from their usual surroundings, but he also juxtaposes their natural calling, which is producing food, killing and being killed. Nature and nurturing are overcome by death and murder. Bäumer does not see enemies in them, only human suffering. These human beings have been transformed into enemies by the signing of a document by some unknown persons. Remarque's statement delineates a theory about the origin of wars as being simply a bureaucratic act that makes people into enemies who are not, thus emphasizing the idiocy of all wars. However, Bäumer does not want to think this thought through as yet; he saves it until the end of the war. The senselessness of war seems to him to be the invitation to a new life after the war, a task worthy of the many years of horror:

> I am frightened: I dare think this way no more. This way lies the abyss. It is not now the time; but I will not lose these thoughts, I will keep them, shut them away until the war is ended. My heart beats fast: this is the aim, the great, the sole aim, that I have thought of in the trenches; that I have looked for as the only possibility of existence after this annihilation of all human feeling; this is a task that will make life afterward worthy of these hideous years. (AQ 196).

Unfortunately, Remarque once again fails to clearly formulate his idea. The reader must complete the notion himself in his own fight against the possibility of such wars occurring again. A clear pacifist statement is lacking, but it may easily be inferred by the reader. Still, this is one of the clearest statements in the book indicating that it was intended to be a pacifist novel.

Back at the front in chapter 9, Bäumer confesses that "this is where I belong" (AQ 203), with his comrades. The emperor arrives to inspect the troops. New, better uniforms are temporarily handed out, and a discussion within the group about the origins of war follows. Although extremely simplistic—after all, the speakers are simple people—Remarque again underscores the insanity of war without, however, coming to any conclusions about its causes. The emperor supposedly did not really want war. Moreover, it is impossible to tell which side is justified. The Germans and French, it is said in the text, both believe that they are only defending their homeland, a view that is confirmed by the intellectuals on both sides. Wars originate because one country insults another (but then, how can one mountain insult another one?). During this war Germans fight against French whom they have never seen before: workers, artisans, and petty civil servants. The implication of these statements is that war does not make any logical sense. Detering comes to the conclusion: "There are other people back behind who profit by the war, that's certain" (AQ 208). With these words Remarque seems to allude to a—very debatable—Marxist explanation that wars are waged for the benefit of the big industrialists. However, Remarque does not pursue this idea. Instead, he describes other possible reasons for war: the prestige and glory for the emperor and the generals, and the war as a kind of fever or disease.

The conclusion is, of course, that there is no such thing as a "better" or "worse" kind of war. Even more important is Remarque's statement: "The national feeling of the soldier resolves itself into this—here [i.e. at the front] he is. But that is the end of it; everything else from joining up onwards he criticizes from a practical point of view" (AQ 209). The mere fact that Remarque does not have his characters realize any "good" reasons for a war also makes the book a pacifist one. The fact that the soldiers are not depicted as fighting from some patriotic feeling, but have been simply drafted and are fulfilling their duty without thinking, was to make the novel appear insulting to the political right wing of the late Weimar Republic. That Remarque does not pursue the potential Marxist argument about the causes of war similarly provoked criticism from the political left wing. Remarque cuts off the discussion by interjecting a statement by Albert: "The best thing is not to talk about the rotten business" (AQ 209). Remarque was reproached by Marxists for not providing a positive perspective. His "heroes" do not want to think, nor do they wish to talk, about war. Perhaps to simple soldiers in their situation that is the way it was, but the fact is that Remarque sees war as accidental, not conditioned by conflicts and constellations of economic interest.

When Bäumer is sent out on patrol, he has an anxiety attack. Only the awareness that he is out there for his comrades whose voices he hears from afar in the trenches fills him with a feeling of warmth and tears him out of his deadly fear. It becomes clear again that he feels close to them because they suffer the same fears and they fear for their lives just as he does. Comradeship as described here then is not so much a love for individual persons as a feeling of community with those who are daily threatened by death.

Bäumer is surprised by a French attack. In a kind of reflex action he stabs the Frenchman who jumps into the shell crater in which he is hiding and witnesses the dying of the man whose death he is personally responsible for. This Frenchman too is addressed as comrade, as a human being, and Bäumer understands that he is just as much a poor devil as he and his comrades are. Bäumer must feel all the more akin to the Frenchman since the latter is a printer, closely related to his own father's profession. And he vows more clearly than anywhere else in the novel to fight "against this, that has struck us both down; from you, taken life—and from me—? Life also. I promise you, comrade. It shall never happen again" (AQ 229). Remarque thus unequivocally confirms the pacifist message of his novel. But we must use caution. The wording is extremely imprecise; the statement is emotional. Bäumer wants to fight against "this." He has never directly or clearly thought about the origins of the war, and he can therefore only advocate a fight without direction and clear goal. Back with his friends, the experience is treated as less important than it was. They tell him that he was just together with the Frenchman for such a long time that the experience had such an enormous effect on him. This does not mean, however, that Remarque wants to discount Bäumer's previous feelings. Rather, he wants to demonstrate the numbing effect that war has—"After all, war is war" (AQ 232). Even feelings of human compassion are annulled by the fight for survival.

After this high point in the action Remarque adds another idyllic scene, which he expressly terms "an idyll of eating and sleeping" (AQ 234). Placed in charge of guarding a food supply depot, the comrades prepare an opulent meal, including roast suckling piglets. Several days later they must vacate the village, and Albert and Bäumer are wounded by shell fragments. The doctor in the field hospital who operates on Bäumer is described as sadistic; and after a train takes Bäumer to an army hospital, another doctor appears who uses the simple soldiers as guinea pigs to operate on their flat feet. Even here the simple soldiers are characterized as dependent and unable to resist the superior powers, in the same way they must obey their superiors at the front.

24

The suffering that Bäumer witnesses in the army hospital is another oc-casion for him to reflect on the nature of the war and its consequences. He thinks how senseless everything is that has ever been written, done, and thought if something as horrible as war is possible. Everything in the world must be a lie and without consequence if thousands of years of culture could not prevent these torrents of blood being spilled, could not prevent hundreds of thousands of these dungeons of torture (hospitals) to exist:

> I am young, I am twenty years old; yet I know nothing of life but de-spair, death, fear, and fatuous superficiality cast over an abyss of sorrow. I see how peoples are set against one another, and in silence, unknow-ingly, foolishly, obediently, innocently slay one another. I see that the keenest brains of the world invent weapons and words to make it yet more refined and enduring. And all men of my age, here and over there, throughout the world, see these things; all my generation is experiencing these things with me. What would our fathers do if we suddenly stood up and came before them and proffered our account? What do they ex-pect of us if a time ever comes when the war is over? Through the years our business has been killing;—it was our first calling in life. Our knowledge of life is limited to death. What will happen afterwards? And what shall come out of us? (AQ 266–67).

All the main themes of the novel may be summarized as follows: the sense-lessness of war; the collapse of the old value system of Western culture and its inability to prevent war; the involvement of the older generation in al-lowing the war to happen and driving the younger generation into war; the young draftees' lack of roots in society; the soldiers' fear with regard to the time spent in the war since they do not know what will become of them later; their fear of not being able to adjust to a normal life, to find their place in society in times of peace since all they know is death and killing. The themes of pacifism, of the senselessness of all wars, and of the lost generation are thus combined without any clear transition. In Remarque/ Bäumer's mind one conditions the other.

As is often the case, this scene of serious reflection is followed by a humorous scene in which the severely wounded Lewandowski makes love to his visiting wife in the hospital bed while the others play a game of skat, a German card game, making sure that the nurses do not interrupt the love-making. It is not surprising that this scene was excluded in older American editions.

The end of the war is near. New transports arrive every day with the wounded from the front line; the makeshift dressings are made out of crepe paper: the German army is failing. Germany cannot even properly care for its wounded and dying soldiers any more. In a short monologue Bäumer relates events of the last few months. After a convalescent leave he is sent back to the front. The fact that his mother does not want to let him return foreshadows his impending death.

Chapter 11 continues the account of events in order to indicate that nothing has changed—the front always remains the same. The soldiers are not counting the weeks any more. It was winter when Bäumer returned to the front line. Now the trees are green, marking the advent of spring, symbolizing hope for a new life. War has become a routine of going back and forth between the front line and the barracks. The soldiers have become dull in their acceptance of war, which now appears to them to be just another cause of death, like cancer or tuberculosis, flu or dysentery. The only difference is that here death occurs more frequently, in a greater number of ways, and in more horrible fashion.

The soldiers feel that together they have formed a brotherhood of comrades trying to survive in an arena of death. Each activity is reduced to a mere act of survival and is therefore restricted to that which is absolutely necessary. Anything else would be a waste of energy. This primitiveness, this regression to bestial behavior, also provides the means for survival, including emotional survival. Entirely in conformity with contemporary vitalism, Bäumer/Remarque then demonstrates the existence of an active life force that has adapted even to this form of reductionism. All other expressions of human emotions are dormant, as the only concern is that life is on a constant watch against the threat of death. Men have turned into animals in order to give them an instinctual weapon; they have become dull in order to prevent a breakdown in face of horrors. If they would give in to clear, conscious thinking, they would surely be unable to face their lives right now. And life has given them the sense of comradeship so that they can escape the abyss of loneliness and abandonment. Thus, once again Remarque emphasizes comradeship as a significant weapon in the soldiers' fight for survival.

This support system is, however, so fragile that it slowly begins to break down. Detering, the farmer, sees the twigs of a cherry tree in bloom and thinks of his farm at home. Without thinking, he deserts right into the arms of the military police. But what would court-martial judges know about his motivations? Detering is never heard of again. The old contrast between front-line experience and the barracks or back home is thus alluded to again. Berger is killed next while trying to save a messenger dog, another example of a lack of logical thinking as the breakdown of inner defenses begins. Müller is killed and Bäumer inherits his boots, although Tjaden was supposed to get them, which clearly indicates Bäumer's impending death.

At this point it has become abundantly clear that Germany cannot win the war. There are too many fresh English and American regiments on the other side, too much corned beef and white flour, and too many new cannons, too many airplanes. The new, ever younger German recruits are dying by the thousands because of lack of military training and experience.

Remarque stresses the heroism of the German soldiers in light of these problems, soldiers who attack time and again in spite of the fact that their front is falling apart: "Is it nothing that regiment after regiment returns again and again to the ever more hopeless struggle, that attack follows attack along the weakening, retreating, crumbling line?" (AQ 279). This is one of the instances in which one could defend Remarque's position against the charges of defeatism and of having smeared the memory of the German soldier. The company leader, Lieutenant Bertinck, who is killed, is described as "one of those superb front-line officers who are in every hot place" (AQ 280). Although Remarque takes great care to show that not all officers are bureaucratic and uncaring about their men, it is interesting that he chooses only the lieutenant, a front-line officer of the lowest rank, as deserving of this praise.

High-ranking officers do not appear in Remarque's novel. Therefore, no reasons for military actions are given or questioned in any way. The group surrounding Bäumer is not a military unit but a unit of friends who simply carry out orders. Seemingly ordered around by anonymous forces, the soldiers have no clear aim. Since the military activities take place without any defined rhyme or reason, their motives themselves are also not questioned or criticized in any way. War is just a dirty, destructive, life-threatening force caused by negligent and stupid politicians. The mechanisms of war cannot be understood by the simple soldier. War is only experienced as a gigantic destructive force against which the soldier fights for survival. He is thus not so much fighting against an enemy as against the anonymous power of war itself—against death. Equating war with death becomes a most pronounced theme in the final section of the novel as the friends die one by one.

Remarque emphasizes that the German soldiers were "not beaten, because as soldiers we are better and more experienced; we are simply crushed and driven back by overwhelmingly superior forces" (AQ 283). He thereby justifies the German defeat and exonerates the soldiers, many of whom, to be sure, would be among his readers. However, this justification does not mean that he subscribes to the right-wing argument that the German army had been stabbed in the back by politicians at home.

Kat is wounded, and Bäumer carries him back to the barracks. When he arrives at the field hospital, Bäumer discovers that Kat is dead, having been hit by a shell splinter in the head while Bäumer was carrying him.

The final chapter is only a little over two pages long. The theme of the lost generation, of the lost youth, and the somewhat pathetic conviction that they will perish, resounds again: "We will be superfluous even to ourselves, we will grow older, a few will adapt themselves, some others will merely submit, and most will be bewildered;—the years will pass by and in the end we shall fall into ruin" (AQ 290). How can it be that youth is gone? Youth is something that Bäumer/Remarque describes as something soft that made their blood restless; it is something uncertain, bewildering, and yet to come; it represents a thousand faces of the future, the melody of dreams and books, the rustling and inkling of what women are all about. Remarque/Bäumer does not want to believe that all of this has been destroyed by artillery barrages, despair, and enlisted men's brothels. Life is still in his own hands and in his eyes.

Looking closely at this description of what lost youth represents, we find that on the one hand it is a yearning for things romantic, for something still to be found in books and thus not real but ideal; on the other hand it constitutes unrealistic expectations with regard to the future, a kind of fulfillment to be derived from a relationship with a woman, presupposing a romantic picture of women which is just as unrealistic. Remarque deplores the loss of innocence that he finds in youth, just as many other writers envision children as symbols for innocence. Clinging to such visions would mean clinging to illusions. To be sure, Remarque makes the aspect of inner destruction more profound by not giving his protagonist the ability to develop more specific ideas about the future and instead having him escape from reality into childhood dreams. On the other hand, we might argue that according to his own biography Remarque himself did not have any more precise ideas. We might also argue that it is not natural for this kind of dreaming to be cut short by the horrors of war. The natural growing process should have been allowed to be more gradual and kinder. However, it is logically just as unjustified to make the war responsible for a necessary maturing process. In his next novel Remarque was to say that education has a similarly negative effect on people. This opinion stems from a romantic notion of what man is supposed to be, a pathetic denial of the necessity of growing up, of adjusting to the realities of adulthood.

In the final two short paragraphs of the book a new narrator is introduced who reports Bäumer's death in a few words. Bäumer was killed in October 1918, on a day that was so quiet on the entire front line that the report in the daily war bulletin was reduced to a single sentence: "All quiet on the Western front." The irony is, of course, that if Bäumer was killed, it was not all quiet on the western front. Thus, Remarque stresses the impersonal character of the killing, the discrepancy between a military point of view and the actual suffering and dying of millions of soldiers, of individual human beings. The title of the book itself thus becomes an accusation, and the entire novel refutes the callous statement of its title: it is not true that it was all quiet on the western front (the literal translation of the German text is "nothing new in the west"). It is incidentally not true that Remarque used a standard phrase of the German army high command. But he did choose a phrase that summarized the cold exigencies of the military value system. This is, also incidentally, the first time in the book that a precise date is given, by reference to the historical daily war bulletin. By taking the change of seasons into consideration, it is possible thus to conclude that the action took place roughly between the summer of 1917 and October 1918.

Remarque does not reveal the identity of the new narrator who gives a seemingly objective report and thus creates a distance between Bäumer and the reader. Yet he does describe the expression on Bäumer's face when he was turned over—a tranquil expression of being almost satisfied that it turned out that way, which makes us believe that this narrator is really one of Bäumer's comrades.

Since the entire preceding narration was first-person narrative, and since Bäumer nowhere in his story explicitly implies that he is writing a diary, this conclusion of the novel does not logically follow from the lost-generation theme. Although Bäumer's death was foreshadowed in numerous ways, it occurs in contrast to the theme of the lost generation, that is, those soldiers, who had escaped the physical destruction of war and remained consequently lost in the society. Thus, the initial statement of the novel can not refer to Franz Bäumer but only to Remarque himself who made himself a spokesperson for the majority of his intended readers, former soldiers of World War I. Given Remarque's tremendous success as a writer, it seems almost ironic that this success is based on the prediction that war destroyed the generation he writes about and made it impossible for them to succeed in real life.

As is obvious from the above quotations, Remarque has tried to write in a simple nonliterary language.[4] He is trying to imitate the normal spoken language of the German front-line soldier with all its repetitive formulas and filler expressions that often say very little, its drastic slang, metaphors and comparisons that often derive their crude humor from references to digestive bodily functions. He thus writes in a style that is the opposite of the Neo-romantic style he used in *Die Traumbude;* indeed, he consciously avoided the somewhat stilted and sophisticated language of literature and used expressions that at the time were considered not acceptable for a literary work of art. The fact that the text is replete with soldiers' jargon identifies the narrator as a simple soldier who speaks the language of the majority of the front-line soldiers. This language, which was so familiar to the majority of the novel's readers, comes across as honest because it does not have the ring of "literature." Remarque thus wants to create the impression that a simple soldier and not a professional writer is giving a truthful report about the war. Through his language the narrator clearly appears as the mouthpiece of millions of soldiers.

This realistic language, however, is often interrupted by soft, lyrical passages which are emotionally charged and which at the same time are reminiscent of the "old," Neo-romantic Remarque of *Die Traumbude* and his early poetry. The following passage may serve as an example:

> The parachute-lights shoot upwards—and I see a picture, a summer evening, I am in the cathedral cloister and look at the tall rose trees that bloom in the middle of the little cloister garden where the monks lie buried. Around the walls are the stone carvings of the Stations of the Cross. No one is there. A great quietness rules in this blossoming quadrangle, the sun lies warm on the heavy grey stones, I place my hand upon them and feel the warmth. At the right-hand corner the green cathedral spire ascends into the pale blue sky of the evening. Between the glowing columns of the cloister is the cool darkness that only churches have, and I stand there and wonder whether, when I am twenty, I shall have experienced the bewildering emotions of love (AQ 119).

The images conjured up in this passage are in stark contrast to the war environment which surrounds Bäumer at that time. At other times, however, similar imagery even serves to romanticize scenes of war. In the above passage it is designed to idealize the memories of early youth and peace in order to underscore the loss of youth brought about by the horrors of war. One might be tempted to criticize Remarque for shifting from one stylistic mode into another, but passages such as the above can easily be explained by attributing them to the former student Bäumer, who had literary ambitions and who was taken directly out of school to be trained as a murderer. Bäumer's education has not endowed him with the ability to rationally question the origin or purpose of war; it is rather the reason for his heightened sensibility.

Other passages that contain strong emotional outbursts and a pathos that seems to contradict the matter-of-factness of a soldier's life with its concentration on survival are like Expressionist prose poems with all their pathetic questioning—for example, the following, which is taken from one of the last pages of the book:

> Summer of 1918—Never has life in its niggardliness seemed to us so desirable as now;—the red poppies in the meadows round our billets, the smooth beetles on the blades of grass, the warm evenings in the cool, dim rooms, the black, mysterious trees of the twilight, the stars and the flowing waters, dreams and long sleep————. O Life, life, life!
>
> Summer of 1918—Never was so much silently suffered as in the moment when we depart once again for the front-line. Wild, tormenting rumours of an armistice and peace are in the air, they lay hold on our hearts and make the return to the front harder than ever.
>
> Summer of 1918—Never was life in the line more bitter and full of horror in the hours of the bombardment, when the blanched faces lie in the dirt and the hands clutch at the one thought: No! No! Not now! Not now at the last moment!
>
> Summer of 1918—Breath of hope that sweeps over the scorched fields, raging fever of impatience, of disappointment, of the most agonizing terror of death, insensate question: Why? Why do they not make an end? And why do these rumors of an end fly about? (AQ 282–83).

The repetition of the phrase "Summer of 1918" marks the individual paragraphs off like stanzas of a poem. The repeated exclamations or rhetorical questions are just as characteristic for Expressionist poetry as its life pathos is for German literature at the turn of the century.

The fact that Remarque presents his novel in small episodes, also typical of all his future novels, made it particularly suitable for serialization. It was easily possible to interrupt the reading and pick it up again with another episode without losing track of the action. The individual episodes can be compared to sequences of a movie, and they considerably facilitated turning Remarque's novels into movies. The episodes that immediately follow each other are often in sharp contrast to each other. Action contrasts with episodes of rest and calm, surprising the reader, creating suspense and at the

31

same time corresponding to the experience of war itself. They are like stones in a mosaic, which only taken together form a whole picture of war. They enable Remarque to highlight only a few experiences, the way they assume importance in the eyes of Bäumer, rather than painting a complete picture in long strokes. The fact that these episodes are only loosely connected or starkly contrasted underscores the fact that Remarque describes only the condition of being at war and not the personal development of his hero.

It is a myth that twelve to fifteen publishers rejected *All Quiet on the Western Front* before it was finally accepted by the publishing house of Ullstein. In point of fact the manuscript was first rejected by Samuel Fischer, the legendary head of Fischer Publishers, because he believed that nobody wanted to read about the war any more; Fischer thought the war experience was something the German nation wanted to forget. Ullstein took a different view; the book was printed in the daily newspaper *Vossische Zeitung* as a serial. Ullstein kept another manuscript ready to substitute for it in case they had to stop printing the novel because of readers' reactions. The opposite happened. During the serialization, from November 10 through December 9, 1928, the *Vossische Zeitung* more than doubled its circulation. With the help of a skillfully launched advertising campaign the book became one of the greatest international successes in publishing history when it appeared in book form on January 31, 1929, under the imprint of the Ullstein Propyläen Verlag. The first edition of 30,000 copies had been printed in advance, and within two months 300,000 had been sold. On May 7, a half million, and after sixteen months a total of one million, copies were sold in Germany alone. For quite some time the publishing firm received orders for 6,000 to 7,000 copies daily. Within a short period of time the novel also became a best-seller abroad. By the end of 1929 it had been translated into twelve languages and a million and a half copies were sold. In the summer of 1930 approximately three million were sold. It is impossible to determine the total number of copies sold worldwide, but in 1952 the author estimated the number to be six million. Others estimated the total number to be twenty to thirty million copies in forty-five to fifty different languages, though more conservative estimates place the number at eight million copies in forty-five languages.

Apart from the publisher's advertising campaign the flood of letters received and published by newspapers and magazines, and the many reviews and articles which ranged from enthusiastic acceptance to total rejection, also contributed to the novel's commercial success. Especially outraged were many conservative groups who claimed that Remarque's characterization of the war was unpatriotic and defeatist. The author himself was also severely attacked. Remarque was said to be not thirty but fifty-five years old. Some claimed that his name was not Remarque but Kramer, Remark read backward and that he was not German but a French Jew, and had never served in the war—and certainly not on the front. In fascist Italy the book was forbidden as early as 1929, and in Germany it was publicly burned in 1933.

Why such uproar about one book? By writing *All Quiet on the Western Front*, Remarque had taken up events and issues the repercussions of which were still decisive in the political situation in Germany. Millions of people could identify with the soldiers' experiences in the novel and saw themselves as one of the characters. Millions were able to use the war as a scapegoat for their own lack of success, their inability to succeed in life. They could blame not their own shortcomings or the political and social situation of contemporary Germany, but the war. For others the war was a high point in their lives, and to see it described as a horrible fight for survival seemed to betray all their youthful patriotic ideals and the ideals of manhood and bravery to which they were clinging in the present. Right-wing political groups such as the Nazis had mythologized World War I and made it the cradle of the spirit of the new Germany which they were envisioning. For them any other view was abhorrent—an insult to the fearless, undefeated German soldier who had been stabbed in the back by his homeland, by those who had started the November 1918 revolution.

Remarque remained rather quiet in all of the public discussions about his book. He gave only a few interviews, in which he claimed that he never intended to write a political book nor one which claimed to make any social or religious statements. He only wanted to report about the individual feelings of a small group of soldiers, mostly former students, during the last two years of the war. Remarque's intention to remain neutral was to no avail. His book had become a political issue, against his will, immediately following its publication. As evidenced by the many different and at times even contradictory political statements in the book and by the superficiality of its argumentation, Remarque was surely not a politically minded person in 1928, and he had no idea that his novel would have such political implications. His protest against war was diffuse and unclear in the text; the war served only as a literary backdrop to the fight for survival of the group of former students and their friends. However, the novel became the testing ground for conflicting political forces within the late phase of the Weimar

Republic. In their fight against the novel and particularly its tremendous success, the various groups of the nationalistic political Right had found a common enemy and were thus able to unite.

In contrast to the reception in Germany, the American reviews of *All Quiet on the Western Front* were all positive. The American reviewers did not have an ax to grind with an author who inherently pleaded for peace, equality, and brotherhood, and as a result they did not attack the author as a pacifist or a traitor to the German cause. This is why they dwelt less on the implied pacifist message of the book, concentrating more on its credibility and ability to convince on a purely human level. It seems as if the description of suffering had completely dominated all political and, to a certain extent, aesthetic considerations. The reviewers praised time and again the book's sincerity, simplicity, honesty, its lack of sentimentality, its realism and economy of style. They overlooked the redolent sentimentality and pathos in the theme of lost youth, and particularly in the scenes involving Paul Bäumer's furlough back home. Also typical of the American reviews were references to other war novels, including Henri Barbusse's *Le Feu* (*Under Fire*, 1916).

Although the American translation of *All Quiet on the Western Front* is no better or worse than most translations, *The New York Times* immediately raised the question of censorship.[5] The president of Little, Brown, and Company, Alfred R. MacIntyre, gave the following explanation in a letter to the *New Republic:*

> When we read the English translation we knew that the book as it stood would offend some people by its frankness, and that under the Massachusetts law, which judges a book not as a whole but by as little as a single phrase, its sale would probably be stopped in Boston. . . . We decided, however, to take this risk, and did no more than delete three words having to do with the bodily functions. We then offered the book to the Book-of-the-Month-Club.[6]

In addition to this minor change, however, three additional passages were left out in the American edition, two of which have been briefly mentioned above: first, several lines referring to the supposed obligation of girls in officers' brothels to wear silk blouses and to take a bath before entertaining guests from a captain upward (AQ 5; first German edition 9); second, one dealing with the German soldiers enjoying sitting on latrines in a meadow and playing a game of cards (almost 3½ pages, AQ 9; first German edition 12–16); third, a scene in the army hospital in Duisburg where a convalescing soldier is having sex with his visiting wife (almost 3½ pages, AQ 267; first German edition 261–64). No censorship had taken place in the British hardcover edition published by Putnam's in 1929. It was not until 1975 that Little, Brown published a new edition based on the complete British edition of 1929.[7] One must add, however, that a letter from Putnam's to Little, Brown and Company of March 21, 1929, had conveyed Remarque's permission "to do what, in your judgement, is in the best interest of the book."[8] It is certain that had Little, Brown not agreed to the cuts, the important advance sale to the Book-of-the-Month-Club would not have materialized.

Remarque was not the first to write a novel about World War I. As is clear from a review that he had written about a number of other war novels, he was intimately familiar with the genre. He simply continued an existing literary trend and gave it a new direction. In doing so, he together with another German writer, Ludwig Renn, whose antiwar novel *Krieg* (War) had appeared in 1928, established a new type of war novel which was later to become popular: The events are reported consistently from the perspective of the simple soldier, and the focus of the action is the events that take place on the front line. All other elements connect directly to these events. Thus, the war novel was changed into a front-line novel, which during the following years was a style adopted by politically right-wing authors.[9]

With regard to Remarque's own literary development *All Quiet* marks a turning point: With *All Quiet on the Western Front* he had found the basic theme for all his later literary works—life threatened by large, overbearing situations, whether they be political forces or deadly diseases. In all his future works the backgrounds change, but the basic underlying principle remains the same.

NOTES

1. "Gespräch mit Remarque," interview with Axel Eggebrecht, *Die literarische Welt* June 14, 1929: 1–2.

2. This is the main argument put forth in a somewhat exaggerated manner by Hans-Harald Müller, *Der Krieg und die Schriftsteller: Der Kriegsroman der Weimarer Republik* (Stuttgart: J. B. Metzler, 1986) 36ff. The most balanced evaluation of the novel is given in the definitive study by Hubert Rüter: *Erich Maria Remarque: Im Westen nichts Neues. Ein Bestseller der Kriegsliteratur im Kontext* (Paderborn: Schöningh, 1980).

3. See, e.g., Alfred Antkowiak, *Erich Maria Remarque: Leben und Werk* (Berlin: Volk und Wissen, 1980).

4. In the following discussion of style and structure I am largely following the analysis of Rüter, 74ff.

5. See Richard Arthur Firda, *Erich Maria Remarque. A Thematic Analysis of His Novels* (New York: Peter Lang, 1988) 58–59.

6. Quoted Firda 59.

7. According to Firda, "a popular Grosset and Dunlap rpt. (New York) published in 1930 was 'complete' and appears to have been based on the London edition" (64).

8. Quoted Firda 59.

9. Rüter 23.

CHAPTER TWO

Inside the Weimar Republic

The Road Back (Der Weg zurück)

In order to write his next book, *The Road Back*, Remarque felt that he had to escape the excitement of Berlin and find a quiet place to work. In December 1929 he returned to Osnabrück, where he rented a quiet apartment in which he could work diligently during the day, leaving him time to visit friends in the evenings. Yet progress was slow, and he left Osnabrück after only four weeks, hoping to return and continue work on his novel the following summer. He was dissatisfied with the version of the novel that had been published in serial form in the *Vossische Zeitung* (December 7, 1930–January 29, 1931) as well as in *Le Matin* (Paris) and *Collier's* in the United States, because in his view the ending was too negative. He therefore kept revising the novel, and as a result the final German edition was not published until April 30, 1931.

The plot of *The Road Back* picks up where *All Quiet on the Western Front* had left off: the last months at the western front, where German troops are fighting their last defensive battles against superior Allied forces. The young Ernst Birkholz is both protagonist and narrator of the novel. After the armistice is signed, Birkholz and his comrades march back to Germany, where they are not very enthusiastically welcomed. Everybody seems to want to forget about the war. Nothing is done by the politicians and local officials to help the soldiers integrate into civilian life. The novel goes on to describe the returning soldiers' inability to find their place in postwar society. Adolf Bethke returns to find that his marriage has been destroyed by his long absence. His wife has had a lover. At first he sends her away, but then takes her back. Under the mounting pressure of the gossipy community Bethke sells his farm and moves to a dingy apartment in the city, where his past continues to haunt him and his wife. Albert Trosske tries to find a place in society together with his girlfriend, Lucie. When he finds her with her lover, he shoots and kills the man and is convicted of second-degree murder. Georg Rahe joins a local *Freikorps*, a kind of volunteer army corps. After participating in putting down the Ruhr District uprisings, he realizes that he is fighting his old comrades and that the old sense of comradeship is gone. He returns to the World War I battlefields in the west, where he commits suicide by shooting himself. Former Lieutenant Ludwig Breyer finds out that he has contracted syphilis during the war, and consequently slits his wrists. Tjaden marries the daughter of a local horse-meat butcher in order to ensure his physical well-being, and Willy Hohmeyer resigns himself to becoming a schoolteacher in a village not far from his hometown. Ernst Birkholz also takes his final exams at the Teachers' Academy, but soon gives up his teaching job in search of something new. Birkholz draws his strength to continue his quest for a meaningful life from nature.

The last months of World War I and the first few years after the war constitute the novel's historical background. At this time the soldiers return to their homeland to find it impoverished by the war effort. Profiting from the economic chaos, from the prevailing hunger and starvation, many got rich overnight from black market trade. Others, poor people, inundated the countryside in a desperate effort to exchange their belongings—durable goods, such as jewelry and furniture—for food from the farmers. The pensions for the many wounded were particularly low, and the country was in political turmoil. Germany was fighting a civil war as the new government tried to defend itself against extremist groups trying to gain power. Re-emerging as a factor in politics, the new German army, the *Reichswehr*, was often used to fight communist uprisings. Also used by the new government were the so-called *Freikorps* (Free Corps), military units of volunteers which consisted of old German army soldiers and new volunteers. Until the signing of the Versailles Treaty these *Freikorps* were under the command of the old German army, and thereafter under the command of the *Reichswehr*.

The *Freikorps* troops were particularly instrumental in putting down uprisings in Bavaria, where in April 1919 a communist *Räterepublik* (Soviet Republic) had been established. In the same year and again in 1920 the *Freikorps* put down communist uprisings in the Ruhr District, where ultimately the *Reichswehr* itself had to step in. In March 1920 ultrarightist forces attempted to take power in Berlin with the help of a *Freikorps*. The revolt collapsed when the *Reichswehr* did not join in, and the workers proclaimed a general strike, triggering uprisings in the Ruhr District and several other similarly unsuccessful revolts all over Germany. Widespread political unrest, mass poverty, an artificial black market economy of newly rich profiteers, as well as the attempt of many people to enjoy life as much as possible characterized life in Germany during the first year after the war. The regime managed to shatter any attempts for a fundamental change on the part of the left. The old forces of the former empire were still alive in practical and ideological terms in both the government and the army.

In the same way as in *All Quiet on the Western Front*, Remarque uses these political and historical forces and events only as the backdrop for his psychological drama. Any specific dates, names of places, or historical events are avoided or only suggested. Remarque did not write a historical novel but a novel in which his protagonists must fight to survive in the face of overwhelming political forces.

By writing *The Road Back*, Remarque set out to prove that his preface to *All Quiet on the Western Front* has prevailed, that the war has destroyed even those young men who escaped its grenades. The fact that *The Road Back* is also a semiautobiographical novel is supported by Remarque's own statement in *The New York Times* ("Remarque to Flee"; September 7, 1929): "In my next book, which I am now writing, I describe the way back to life, how a young man like myself—and Paul Bäumer— experienced war as a youth, who still carries its scars and who was then grabbed up by the chaos of the post-war period. He finally finds his way back into life's harmonies." The city that Remarque describes in *The Road Back* also clearly resembles Osnabrück. Birkholz's experiences are to a large extent the same as Remarque's own—particularly his return to school, passing the teacher's exam, and teaching in a small village nearby. Descriptions of the beauty of nature evoked in the novel are reminiscent of Remarque's own memories of the canal where he used to fish as a boy.

The book begins with an introductory chapter describing the western front and the end of the World War I hostilities. Winter is on its way, marking the time clearly as fall of 1918. When suddenly the guns fall silent, the soldiers have an uncanny feeling. They feel much more at ease when they hear the roaring big guns and the hammering machine guns again. The world of war and death has become their world. Peace makes them feel uncomfortable, and when the birth of a peaceful world draws near, the comrades express their apprehensions about the great silence: "Yes, that's it, the dregs" (RB 20). The front and the world of dying have become their home; this is where their life is, where their comrades have died, and where they belong. Herein lies the main theme of the book: that during the war true manly values were realized in comradeship, in caring for each other, risking one's life for one another, when social differences and money did not matter. Remarque goes on to describe the reestablishment of bourgeois values, social differences, and the gradual destruction of comradeship. An uncaring world makes it impossible for many soldiers to find their place in society and forces them to commit suicide or lead an unfulfilled life. Peace becomes in many ways worse than war.

Part 1 of the novel describes the soldiers' march home and their subsequent arrival in the town. On the way they meet well-nourished and well-equipped American soldiers, who are younger than the group of friends but older than the young new recruits. They feel sorry for the German soldiers whose wounds are dressed with paper bandages. Soon a new sense of comradeship is established between the groups, and the men turn out to be natural businessmen and begin to barter. The fact that all soon become friends tacitly questions why these people fought each other in the war. When Max Weil, a Jewish soldier, brings the news that a revolution has broken out in Berlin and the emperor has fled to the Netherlands, the soldiers' reaction is one of disbelief, and the feeling of having been betrayed. To provide a contrast to the descriptions of fighting, revolution, and comradeship, Remarque interjects scenes that are full of normal, everyday life. A sexual encounter with young girls in a country inn and a romantic image of a field in which potatoes are roasted in ashes evoke the feeling of a returning youth; life seems to have triumphed over death.

This triumph is, however, only fleeting. This vitalism and intimations of a returning lost youth are only momentary whispers. Remarque creates these short scenes of hope only to make the following disillusionment greater. In a discussion between Lieutenant Heel and Max Weil two fundamental views collide: The officer believes in heroism and lofty values that are worth dying for and Weil believes in the quiet heroism of humanity and love; the death of millions cannot be justified. ("The misery of millions is too big a price to pay for the heroics of a few" [RB 49]). Remarque maintains that the world will not change from all this talk and is skeptical about the value of mere words. Just as in *All Quiet on the Western Front* he rejects intellectual analysis. At the end of Part 1, he describes a long train ride home in which references are made to revolution and loneliness. This contrasts sharply to the previously described sense of comradeship and foreshadows bad things to come.

Part 2 describes the first encounters with the world in the hometown up until the point when Ernst Birkholz returns to school. Remarque's negative opinion of the November Revolution is revealed in an encounter with the revolutionary sailors. The soldiers at the front are contrasted with the sailors who have been sitting on their boats and doing nothing during the war. Now they want to attack the front soldiers. Later in the novel he refers to the November Revolution as a wind skimming over the water and creating ripples; not penetrating its surface for any deeper effect. Since the conservative government officials remained in power in Germany, the "revolutionary wind" has had no lasting impact. Remarque has Georg Rahe say that this revolution was started by party secretaries who fought each other within various leftist groups while at the same time the rightists were killing them off. It is little wonder that Remarque's disbelief in the power of revolution and his disregard for the political forces on the extreme left has, in this novel too, met with sharp criticism from Marxist scholars.

Remarque's protagonist, Ernst Birkholz, cannot understand the concerns of his own family any more; they appear trivial to him in comparison to what he had experienced at the front. Birkholz does not want to be treated like a child; he does not want to be reprimanded by his father for smoking, or, as described later in the novel, scolded by his mother for using crude language. Birkholz's friend Willy cannot understand why his mother is outraged by his stealing and killing the neighbor's rooster, the kind of action that became second nature to him at the front. This incident is exaggerated and artificially constructed, and seems to be included only to demonstrate the point that there are different moral values at the front than at home. A much more believable scene in which Willy and Ernst Birkholz mistake the howling of an electric streetcar for an approaching shell and try to take cover also demonstrates the hold that wartime habits still have on them. But, unfortunately, by and large the examples are too obviously chosen to demonstrate the discrepancy between the former soldiers and their old/new world at home. The novel is too crudely constructed, and the examples are too artificial and extreme, to be convincing.

The comrades join a demonstration against the government in which the people express hopes for a new world, hopes that are crushed by the bureaucrats' speeches. Parallel to the beating of Himmelstoss in *All Quiet on the Western Front* is the scene in which a former sergeant named Seelig is beaten by the group of friends. Seelig is now an innkeeper who seems to have forgotten his behavior during the war, thus providing another example of the fact that the world has changed since the war. Any attempts to try to come to terms with the changed society and wartime experiences fail—as, for example, the Lieutenant Breyer's futile attempt to come to terms with his experiences by reading books.

At a rich uncle's home Birkholz makes a fool of himself when he picks up a pork chop with his hands at the dinner table, demonstrating the clash between wartime experiences and peacetime social norms. At the same dinner party guests arrogantly muse about the fact that the president of the

Reich, Friedrich Ebert, is a harness maker by trade. In contrast to this arrogance Birkholz remembers what a good soldier Adolf Bethke had been. This contrasting scene again underscores the differences of the two value systems. The conservative guests at the dinner party maintain that the war could have been won in another two months, thus supporting the notorious *Dolchstoßlegende*—the legend of an undefeated German army stabbed in the back at home by Jews and communists, a legend popular among many conservatives during the Weimar Republic.

The way the former soldiers now view their teachers has also changed: they now have only contempt for the older men. When the director of the old school makes a pathetic speech about the heroism of the troops and romanticizes the many who sacrificed themselves for the fatherland, the students cut him off with an account of the horrible realities of war. Once again Remarque—in a similarly pathetic tone—insists that one should not talk about one's war experiences any longer. Part 2 closes with a rhetorical question about whether these returning soldiers are now able to cope during peacetime.

The answer to this question as developed in the following sections of the novel is a clear no. Adolf Bethke's wife has been unfaithful to him, a situation that stems from the long separation during the war and that he is in no way equipped to deal with. Life at the front seems to be simple in comparison to the complicated life he is confronted with in peacetime society. The only element of this society that Birkholz values at this point, comradeship, cannot overcome the current social problems. Birkholz feels estranged and alone, tries to recapture the spirit of his youth by going fishing in the canal, but he can look at the familiar landscape only through the eyes of the soldier who needs to take cover and defend himself.

Part 4 could have been entitled "Disappointments." The rift between soldiers and civilians has become wider. The returning soldiers thought that their new life would be filled with a strong and intensive awareness of their own existence. These hopes, which were shared by an entire generation, were crushed. Karl Bröger sells his library in order to become a liquor dealer, an act fraught with symbolic significance. Many people have undergone a quick change in their attitude to each other. Valentin, a former acrobat and a courageous soldier, meets the now successful black marketeer Ledderhose, who pretends not to remember their shared war experiences. A similar incident occurs a few pages later when Valentin meets with another well-dressed former comrade. When describing an evening gathering at Waldmann's bar, where there is nightly dancing, Remarque demonstrates another aspect of the Weimar years; the attempt of many to escape reality and enjoy life by having as much fun as possible. Birkholz meets his old girlfriend Adele again, but she soon breaks up the relationship. She has changed and so has he; their youth cannot be recaptured, and when Birkholz says good-bye to Adele, he symbolically also says good-bye to his youth. During the first reunion of the old regiment it becomes very clear that the social class system has reemerged and has destroyed the soldierly sense of comradeship. The father's profession, family heritage, and their very clothing separate those who belong together from those who do not. The common bonds of the former comrades are broken, and each must go his way alone. Georg Rahe joins a *Freikorps* unit in order to recapture the old spirit of comradeship and escape the new world of purposefulness for a life regulated by order, duty, and regularity. In his eyes peace has become a war of each person against everyone else.

Part 5 accurately describes Remarque's own experiences as a teacher in small villages through the eyes of Birkholz. Birkholz cannot find fulfill-ment in the arms of a little seamstress, where he feels even more alone than by himself. Nor does he feel fulfilled as a teacher, believing that he cannot teach anything to these children who alone remained innocent in all those war years. In the face of the atrocities of war he does not believe in the benefit of education any more. When Birkholz wants to write a word be-ginning with a к on the blackboard, he automatically writes Kemmelberg, the name of the place where many died in the war. His memories keep intruding into the present. Whereas his friend Willy is content with the simple life in the countryside, the reflective Birkholz leaves the teaching profession, just as Remarque did.

Ending in suicide and murder, Part 6 marks the end of the old comrade-ship. The Roaring Twenties are in full swing as newer and more sophisti-cated amusement establishments open up. In contrast Remarque describes a large demonstration of starving and crippled war veterans. Before the city hall army troops under the command of a former comrade shoot a demon-strator who wants to prevent bloodshed. It is Weil who is killed in the name of law and order, the old sense of comradeship killed by machine gun fire. Similarly, when another member of the old group of friends, Albert, kills the man who has taken away his girlfriend, he simply reacts as he would have in the war. Ludwig Breyer, on the other hand, kills himself not only because he has contracted syphilis during the war, but also out of despera-tion because his romantic feelings of youth are gone forever. In reporting Breyer's suicide, Remarque breaks away from his narrative perspective and writes from the standpoint of an omniscient narrator. Because of Breyer's suicide, Birkholz has a nervous breakdown.

Part 7 opens with a description of Birkholz's recovery after weeks of being ill as he turns his attention to the beauties of nature. The reference to nature foreshadows his return to life as he gains a more positive outlook on his present life and hope for the future. Georg Rahe has left the *Freikorps*, disillusioned after seeing the uniforms of the workers he had helped kill in the Ruhr District revolts. He realized that he was killing his own former comrades in a civil war. Following this realization, Rahe returns to the old battlefields at the former western front and shoots himself. At this point, Remarque again deviates from Birkholz's perspective as a narrator and presents an omniscient narrator. Birkholz participates in Albert's defense in court; he and his comrades appear as witnesses and accuse society of having taught Albert to kill.

At the conclusion of the novel Remarque summarizes the main theses: the old comradeship is dead, and the optimism of a romantic youth has collapsed in the barrages of 1917. There is a fear that the new generation is preparing for a new war; Birkholz, Willy, and Kosole witness a group of boys playing war games in the forest. It is interesting that Remarque refers to the adult leader of the patriotic group as their *Führer*, clearly identifying them as a rightist youth group and foreshadowing the later Hitler Youth. The experience triggers an inner change in Birkholz: he now looks forward to returning to his village as an instructor to teach his students about, as his friend Willy put it, "real love of one's homeland" (RB 340). He has overcome the dark shadows of his past and has found a new task in his life, limited as it may be. Images of nature, of growing and blossoming, confirm his positive viewpoint.

Obviously this happy ending is artificially attached to a predominantly negative novel. It is also obvious that the entire novel is highly fabricated; episodes serve primarily as examples to demonstrate typical behavior. Remarque repeats his points over and over again, and each thesis is proven ten times over. Yet in writing *The Road Back*, Remarque succeeded in demonstrating that he was an author capable of writing more than one novel. The war scenes at the beginning are at least as convincing and well-written as those in *All Quiet on the Western Front*. The scenes in Birkholz's home correspond to the furlough scenes in *All Quiet on the Western Front*. The description of the estrangement of the returning soldiers from the world of the early 1920s is psychologically convincing, although there are so many examples that an overkill results.

Many German reviews picked up these positive elements, although it was clear that the book did not measure up to *All Quiet on the Western Front*, and it owed its much more modest sales to the reputation of its forerunner. Many other German reviewers scolded the author for not taking a clear political stand. Most American reviews, on the other hand, were surprisingly positive, even when they compared the book to *All Quiet on the Western Front*. Some critics judged it, indeed, an even better novel. Apparently the American reviewers valued the book for its inherent humanistic message, not for its possible political implications and arguments. Some reviewers rightfully pointed out the artificiality of the characters and the calculated effects of the rather simplistically constructed stories.

Three Comrades (*Drei Kameraden*)

It was not until December 1936 that Remarque was able to complete his next novel, *Three Comrades*, a project that he had begun in 1932 and which underwent a number of revisions before it was published. The American edition appeared on April 26, 1937. An edition in German appeared in 1938, published by the Dutch Querido Verlag, publisher of many exile writers. After the invasion of the Netherlands by the German army in May 1940, Querido was no longer able to distribute the book. Quite aside from that, the sales figures of all German editions of Remarque's books were small from 1933 through 1945, due to the loss of the Third Reich market.

Three Comrades is in many respects a continuation of the preceding two novels, and although Remarque never intended it as such, it may be considered the final part of a trilogy. It is set in Berlin during the Weimar era around the year 1928. Although he later wrote another novel set in the Weimar Republic, *The Black Obelisk*, *Three Comrades* marks the end of Remarque's concern with the World War I soldiers' reentry into postwar society. The protagonist and first-person narrator of *Three Comrades* is Robert Lohkamp (Robby), who works for his old war buddy and company commander Otto Köster in his automotive repair shop. Gottfried Lenz, the third of the "three comrades," is called the "Last Romantic." As a fourth comrade one could add "Karl," an automobile that Köster, a racing fanatic, has made into a race car, though maintaining its outward unsightly appearance. One of the three friends' main pastimes is to challenge unsuspecting owners of modern and better looking automobiles on the highway to a race and thus show off Karl's hidden power. On one such occasion they meet Patricia (Pat) Hollmann, a young girl whom Robby fancies and consequently courts. The two become lovers, and this love temporarily takes Robby away from the dreariness of his boardinghouse furnished room, his drinking bouts, and his evenings spent as a piano player in a local brothel. Thus, Pat becomes the real "fourth comrade" as Remarque adds a romantic love element to the theme of comradeship based on a bond established during war.

Business seems to be going tolerably well for the three friends, although their ventures are constantly on the verge of financial ruin. But then, during an idyllic vacation at the coast, Pat's tuberculosis that lay dormant for many years begins to flare up. Comradeship proves itself on this occasion: when Robby calls Otto Köster, he manages to drive in a medical expert from Berlin in record time to see Pat. When fall comes Pat must leave the northern German climate and go to a sanatorium in the Alps where the patients lead an artificial existence in the face of impending death. The atmosphere in the sanatorium is reminiscent of Thomas Mann's novel *The Magic Mountain* (1924), which doubtless influenced Remarque. After going to a political rally, Gottfried is shot and killed in the street by a member of a proto-Nazi group, though Remarque is careful not to directly identify it as such. Gottfried's death is avenged by another friend, Alfons, before Köster is able to get to the murderer. Robby spends the last weeks before Pat's death together with her in a kind of bittersweet, *carpe diem* existence, financially supported by Köster, who even sells his car Karl. The sale of Karl represents the ultimate proof of friendship for Robby. After Pat's death Robby has little to return to, and Köster's auto repair shop is also financially near bankruptcy. All the equipment is auctioned off.

The time of *Three Comrades* can fairly exactly be pinpointed to 1928. At one point Gottfried talks about having left Rio de Janeiro in 1924, and at another point an old Mercedes Benz car is referred to as being a 1923 vintage. Although there are a great number of unemployed, the economic crisis of 1929 has not yet taken place. It is the time of the final stages of the Weimar Republic. During the elections of May 20, 1928, the government parties suffered heavy losses, and the Communists and Social Democrats formed a coalition government which was hated by the liberal and rightist parties. The years of economic expansion, made possible by the influx of predominantly American capital, are coming to an end. People are trying to enjoy life as much as possible and to forget the misery in which they live. The economy is showing signs of the approaching depression. While some entrepreneurs still prosper and drive big American and German cars, the number of unemployed is rapidly increasing. At one point the unemployed are shown betting their last money on horse races: one of them collapses in the betting offices. In another scene Robby takes Pat to a museum which, to his amazement, is crowded. As it turns out, the crowds mostly consist of the unemployed, who spend their winter idle time in the warm museum. Whitecollar workers are especially hard hit by the developing economic crisis. They work many overtime hours without pay, as, for example, Robby's neighbor Hasse, hoping not to be fired. For economic reasons suicides are commonplace, and shootings in the streets occur daily. It is also a time during which the political parties on the right and left gained ardent followers, leading to political rallies that had to be broken up by the police. Remarque describes several such political meetings—without, however, identifying the political parties he is talking about. We can only assume that one of them, run by party secretaries, is either a Communist or a Social Democratic meeting, while another one, at which many empty promises are made, is a National Socialist rally. As previously noted, Remarque is careful not to state which party Gottfried's killer belongs to, merely mentioning that he was wearing a uniform and yellow leather leggings.

One of the reasons why Koester does not want to leave the killer up to the police is the historical fact that during this time killers from the political right often received extremely light sentences. But just as in the case of Albert Trosske in *The Road Back* there are other reasons as well: Remarque's heroes take a kind of personal revenge. Köster has learned to kill in the war. He remembers when he killed a young English fighter pilot, and he feels that this killing would only be justified if he also kills the man who shot Gottfried Lenz, surely a questionable logical conclusion. The same kind of logic is applied when Robby almost beats a porter to death, a mean and despicable character who had beaten him up when he was defenseless. This act of revenge is more than getting even for the injustice done to him. It is rather that this person seems to be enjoying the best of health while his girlfriend Pat is suffering from tuberculosis and will soon die. Thus he confuses his anger with his grievance, although he feels "much better" afterward.

The intensity of nationalist emotions increases, and Remarque's own aversion toward nationalism becomes indirectly clear when he describes one of the other boarders on Robby's corridor refusing to apologize for his rude treatment of a Russian by stating that a German man does not apologize— particularly not to an Asian. As always in his novels Remarque condemns fanaticism and extremism in every form, no matter what political ideology it is inspired by. Robby once remarks to Köster that in his opinion the people who attend the big party rallies do not want politics, they want a substitute religion; Köster replies that people just want to believe in something, no matter what. Remarque thus is not concerned with specific political ideologies but with the general cause of unrest: the religious and political loss of faith experienced by his generation during the war years.[1]

During the late years of the Weimar Republic many people had a great admiration for technology, for car races such as the ones Karl and his owner participate in. It was also a time of admiration for things American, as evidenced by the number of American cars that appear in the novel. Yet one must again bear in mind that Remarque did not write a historical novel, since the political events of the late 20s play only a minor role, with perhaps the exception of Gottfried's shooting. The Weimar Republic serves only as a backdrop of turmoil and confusion for the personal reactions and philosophies of Remarque and his characters.

This novel also contains a considerable number of autobiographical elements. Like Remarque, Robby was drafted in 1916 when he was eighteen years old. Since at the time of the action he is roughly thirty years old, this confirms the date of 1928. In 1917 he arrived in Flanders as a soldier. In 1918 he was wounded and taken to a field hospital. Shortly after the war his mother died from cancer, and in 1923 he became publicity manager for a rubber manufacturer. Like Remarque, Robby plays the piano well enough to be employed as a piano player in a brothel. Robby gave Pat an Irish terrier by the name of Billy so that she would never have to be alone, just as Remarque gave an Irish terrier of the same name to his first wife, Jeanne Zambona. Furthermore, there is no doubt that Jeanne Zambona served as the model for the character Pat. Not only does the description of her physical appearance fit perfectly, but like Pat, Jeanne Zambona also had contracted tuberculosis, presumably as the result of malnutrition during and immediately after the war, and she repeatedly had to spend time in a sanatorium in Switzerland. However, whereas in Zambona's case her disease could be arrested and controlled when it reoccurred, in Pat's case it could not. It is futile however, to speculate why Remarque deviated from his autobiographical model—whether or not, for example, he put "a symbolic end to the most significant love of his life."[2] The reason for Pat's death within the context of the novel is clear: love and happiness cannot exist in such perilous times.

The fact that Remarque dedicated his novel to "J. R. Z." (Jeanne Remarque Zambona) can only be interpreted as an expression of his deep feelings for his first wife, although they had already been legally divorced.

Perhaps Remarque celebrated his relationship to Jeanne Zambona in the novel as an ideal relationship between a man and a woman. The fact that Pat dies and that she is characterized as a *femme fragile* with a kind of moribund beauty not only connects her type with many similar characters found in German turn-of-the-century literature, for example in the work of Thomas Mann; it also characterizes her as a type of woman who could hardly be considered a typical German *Hausfrau*.

In *Three Comrades* the political turmoil and societal problems of the rapidly declining Weimar Republic have taken over the World War I themes and the early postwar years of the two previous novels. The times are characterized as being ruled by extreme matter-of-factness. In Robby's and his friends' eyes everything is useless, pointless, and dirty—there is nothing worth living for. There is no security, no permanence, and therefore one must always live with the awareness that everything may collapse at any moment. The twentieth century is so absurd, so ridiculous, that one can only laugh at it. Thus, humor becomes a weapon of self-defense. Robby and his friends are engaged in a constant fight for survival. When a brawl erupts between them and a rival auto repair shop as to who has the right to tow away and repair a car that has been in an accident, this fight symbolically becomes a struggle for survival, a mirror of similar situations in a society that is like a war of all against all. The absurdity of the social conditions also reveals itself in the political fights between the rival political parties and factions, in street fights and shootings. Consequently, Robby feels that going to the theater is too bourgeois; it is pointless since contemporary politics with their shootings offer enough real "theater."

This negative view of society is confirmed by a very realistic, vivid description of the characters in Robby's boardinghouse: the private secretary who has a conspicuously high life style because she is more than just a secretary to her boss: the student who has worked in a mine in order to attend the university but who cannot make it financially, so that all his efforts turn out to be futile; the nationalistic public official and formerly harmless stamp collector who allows himself to be indoctrinated; the nurse whose two children died from starvation during the war years; the honest white-collar worker who is always afraid of being fired and who commits suicide when he discovers that his wife is cheating on him; the Russian emigré who is a professional dancing partner at a local café and who hopes some day to find a job as receptionist in a decent hotel. Other typical characters include the humane and likable Jewish businessman who buys the Cadillac from Robby and later sells it back to him, the master baker and widower who is being manipulated by his new wife, and the classical whores with the good hearts. Although some of these are stock characters of other literary traditions, together they still accurately represent the Weimar Republic society. This society characterized by Remarque is the image of humanity trying to struggle for survival in a world gone haywire.

When we meet Robby and his comrades at the beginning of the novel, Remarque seems to blame their lack of success and their inability to find a place in society not only on financial but also on human factors having to do with their war experiences. We are again confronted with a group of characters similar to Hemingway's heroes of the lost generation in *The Sun Also Rises*. Nothing matters to them any more except survival. Hard liquor helps them to forget, and it is here that we find for the first time what later becomes a trademark of Remarque's novels: the excessive consumption of alcoholic beverages. It may be speculated that this reflects the author's own life style. Robby's friend Valentin Hauser gets drunk every day to celebrate his survival during the war; another of his friends, the painter Ferdinand Grau, who makes his living by painting portraits of deceased people, drinks because he has resigned himself to the fact that "we all must die" (TC 215). Robby's older friends, Gottfried and Otto,—they lovingly refer to Robby as the "baby"—have already given up; there is no hope for fulfillment in life for them any more, but they support Robby in his fight for happiness. Although both of them are also in love with Pat, they prod Robby to court her, because they feel that only he still has the chance to gain happiness in life.

Beauty of life and happiness in love are realized as being only temporary, as fleeting phenomena. One must nevertheless fight for them, must fight for the few things one loves. Fighting is necessary, because if you do not give up, you are victorious over fate—ideas that remind us very much of Hemingway. Thus, Robby fights for a life with Pat and for Pat's life, because in his view everything would be pointless if Pat should die. Since at the end Pat does indeed die, we can only view this outcome as a negative judgment on the chances of Remarque's heroes finding meaning in life. Thus *Three Comrades* clearly represents a step back from the seemingly optimistic ending of *The Road Back*, where man's relationship with nature leads the protagonist toward regeneration. *Three Comrades* is characterized by an atmosphere of isolation and loneliness in which the protagonists attempt to find meaning in life and lose in each case. Lenz tries politics and is killed. Köster for a while finds meaning in his devotion to his car which he is forced to sell for his friend, and Robby seemed to have found it in his love for Pat who dies. Death itself destroys the group of friends so that in the end only two out of four characters are left.

The theme of the lost generation is carried over from Remarque's first two novels. There are also clear references to *All Quiet on the Western Front* and its heroes when Robby remembers, among others, Kaczinsky, Kemmerich, and Berger, and comes to a gloomy conclusion regarding God's goodness and the help he gives to man. Remarque's judgment about the world is equally pessimistic: "The details are wonderful, but the whole has no sense. As if it had been made by a madman who could think of nothing better to do with the marvellous variety of life that he created but to annihilate it again" (TC 471).

The only positive things in the world are happiness, love, and beauty as personified in Pat. Since these do not last, their transitoriness is also proof of the senselessness of human existence. When Pat becomes ill, Robby thinks: "She must come through . . . else all is filth" (TC 249). But there is another, more positive aspect which also forms a link with the two previous novels: the concept of comradeship. This comradeship truly does prove itself in the novel, particularly when Pat is sick and urgently needs a doctor. Robby's ability to rely on his comrades when he is at the seacoast resort, his inner knowledge that he is not alone because he has his comrades and knows that they will help him, is an exact parallel to Paul Bäumer's feelings during his lonely patrol in front of the trenches in *All Quiet on the Western Front*. This comradeship does indeed last to the very end. However, two of the four comrades, Pat and Lenz, die, one a victim of malnutrition during the war, the other one a victim of the political turmoil during the late Weimar years. Although the feeling of individual responsibility for the fellow comrades does survive, they are broken apart as a result of the political turmoil of the times.

Remarque's style in *Three Comrades* suffers a bit from the mannered comparisons betraying his strained attempts to impress his readers. This is the first novel in which Remarque's tendency to become melodramatic borders on tastelessness. His description of Pat's final days at the sanatorium is, however, one of the best episodes he has written. There is a certain carry-over of some of the pathetic aspects of his previous novels, as, for example, when Robby remembers how they wanted to march against egotism and lies immediately after the war:

> We had meant to wage war against the lies, the selfishness, the greed, the inertia of the heart that was the cause of all that lay behind us; we

had become hard, without trust in anything but in our comrades beside us and in things—the sky, trees, the earth, bread, tobacco, that never played false to any man,—and what had come of it? All collapsed, perverted and forgotten (TC 60).

Remarque evokes pathos when describing Robby supposedly belonging to a kind of secret order of the unsuccessful with desires and no goals, with love without a future, and desperation without reason. There is no doubt that such proclamations have a hollow ring, just as does the glorification of manliness through drinking and fistfights. The novel is saturated with the kind of sentimentality so typical of the so-called New Objectivity movement, the style of many German writers of the late 20s and early 30s. Although in *Three Comrades* Remarque has written his first great love story as a tribute to his first wife, he exhausted the themes of the lost generation and comradeship.

Since the novel could not be published in Germany, nothing can be said about its reception in Remarque's home country. The most striking feature of the American reviews is that *Three Comrades* was no longer being compared to *All Quiet on the Western Front*; it seems that either enough time had passed to judge Remarque's new books on their own merits, or that the subject matter was so radically different that a comparison did not suggest itself. Although no one grumbled about the excessive sentimentality of the love story—the movies of the late 30s and 40s were replete with this element—several American reviewers again criticized the book's lack of political significance. It was obviously time for Remarque to choose a different subject matter, one that had closer connection to his own time and its political events.

NOTES

1. Christine R. Barker and R. W. Last, *Erich Maria Remarque* (London: Oswald Wolff, 1979) 85.

2. Harley U. Taylor, Jr., *Erich Maria Remarque: A Literary and Film Biography* (New York: Peter Lang, 1989) 110.

CHAPTER THREE

The Exile Writes on Exile

Flotsam (*Liebe deinen Nächsten*)

As he was himself an exile, it is little wonder that Remarque made exile or, more specifically, the plight of refugees from Nazi Germany the main topic of his next two novels, *Flotsam* (1941) and *Arch of Triumph* (1946). He took up this theme again later in his last two novels, *The Night in Lisbon* and *Shadows in Paradise*.

Although Remarque wrote all his books in German, the first edition of *Flotsam* was in English, translated by Denver Lindley and published in 1941 in America. A German edition was published the same year in Sweden by the exile publishing firm Bermann-Fischer, who had taken over the publication of German exile authors previously published by Querido of Amsterdam.

In contrast to Remarque's earlier novels the exile novels are narrated from a third-person perspective, which creates a greater distance to the story as well as giving the impression of being more objective. *Flotsam* has two distinct protagonists: an older one called Josef Steiner, who is experienced in the art of survival, and a young man by the name of Ludwig Kern. Some time before Austria is annexed to Germany in 1938, Kern meets Steiner during a police raid in a cheap Vienna boardinghouse for refugees. Together with many other refugees they are arrested and taken to prison. Neither one has a valid passport, residence, or work permit. The twenty-one-year-old Kern had left Germany because he is half-Jewish and was not permitted to continue his studies at the university. He had tried to make a living by illegally selling soaps and perfumes from door to door. Steiner had fled from a German concentration camp, but his wife was still in Germany. He becomes Kern's teacher in the art of survival as a refugee.

After his release from prison two weeks later, Kern is sent to Czechoslovakia. In Prague he falls in love with the young Ruth Holland, a former student, of Jewish extraction, whom he later meets again in Vienna. Steiner now works at the great Viennese amusement park, the Prater, where he is able to secure a job for Kern too. When Kern goes to meet Ruth outside the university where she has resumed her studies, he gets involved in a fight between Jewish and non-Jewish students and ends up in jail again. In the meantime Ruth is forced to leave the country and goes to Zurich; Kern also crosses the border and meets her in Switzerland. He is arrested after he tries to get some money from a German by the name of Ammers who turns out to be a Nazi.

In the meantime, Steiner has left Austria in anticipation of the German annexation (1938). When he receives a letter from his wife, who is dying from cancer in a German hospital, he goes back to Germany to be with her. He is denounced by the nurse and arrested by the Gestapo officer Steinbrenner, who had previously tortured him. When Steiner walks down the stairs together with Steinbrenner, he pushes him out of the window and jumps out with him to his death. With the help of the Refugees' Aid Committee, Kern and Ruth, who in the meantime have also arrived in Paris, manage to get a visa and entry permit to go to Mexico, and thus get a chance to begin a new life.

Here again some explanation of the historical events is warranted. Shortly after the National Socialists' rise to power on January 30, 1933, the floodgates opened for thousands of refugees to flee Nazi Germany. The majority of these refugees were being persecuted, or at least were in danger for political, religious, or racial reasons, especially Jews, Communists, Social Democrats, all those politically opposed to Hitler, as well as members of the National Socialist Party who disagreed with Hitler's specific political program in some minor way. The exodus included many of Germany's leading scientists, scholars, writers, and artists. Most of the refugees first went to neighboring countries, particularly Czechoslovakia, Austria, and Switzerland, where German was spoken; but after Austria was united with the German Reich in March 1938, and after Czechoslovakia had been taken in March 1939, more and more refugees went on to Switzerland and France. When Hitler's troops finally marched into France in May 1940 after Poland had been defeated in the fall of 1939, many refugees continued on to Great Britain, Sweden, the United States, or to Central and South America, often via Spain and Portugal.

During the 1930s, the time Remarque's first two exile novels take place, public acceptance of the refugees by their host countries had been complicated by employment laws during the depression. These laws prevented foreigners from holding most kinds of jobs. The laws were originally designed to prevent the influx of foreign workers so as to protect the home economy. They now worked against the refugees, who were denied residence and working permits and consequently sent across the border to other neighboring countries.

The refugees included a high percentage of Jews. For example, at least 80 percent of the immigrants registered between 1933 and 1945 in the United States as Germans, Austrians, and Poles were Jews. According to the Swiss authorities almost all immigrants and refugees who arrived after the beginning of World War II were Jews or descendants of Jews. Approximately 90,000 Jewish refugees had arrived in the United States by late 1941, and many others went to South America and Palestine. Of the 502,799 Jews who were residing in the German Reich on January 1, 1933, approximately 270,000 emigrated between 1933 and 1941. The numbers are much larger for countries that were occupied by the Germans during World War II. The number of non-Jewish emigrés is estimated at about 300,000, including approximately 45,000 Communists. The majority of the Communists went via Czechoslovakia and Scandinavia to the Soviet Union. The number of Social Democratic emigrés is estimated at 3,000. It is interesting to note that most of the refugees did not join any political exile organizations. Since many internationally famous people had to flee Germany, including such luminaries as the founder of psychoanalysis, Sigmund Freud; physicist Albert Einstein, writers Thomas and Heinrich Mann and Bertolt Brecht, composer Paul Hindemith, conductors Bruno Walter and Otto Klemperer—7,622 intellectuals emigrated to the United States alone—this drain of German intellectual life represented a tremendous intellectual and moral loss of prestige for Hitler Germany.

Since anti-Semitism was an integral part of National Socialist ideology, the persecution of Jews in Germany began as early as April 1, 1933, with a boycott of all Jewish businesses. The infamous Nuremberg Laws of 1935 robbed Jews of their German citizenship, and during the *Kristallnacht* ("Crystal Night," November 9, 1938) Jewish-owned stores were looted and synagogues burnt. Jews were excluded not only from public service jobs but also from the professions. They were not allowed to play any role in the economic life of Germany; they had to report all their financial assets and could no longer acquire or freely sell real estate. They were not allowed to attend public schools and universities and could not marry non-Jews. Their passports and identification cards were specially stamped with a *J*, and if they chose to emigrate, they had to pay a special tax and were allowed to take very little along with them. After 1941 all Jews had to wear a yellow Star of David labeling them as Jews, and after June 1942 the systematic annihilation of Jews in death camps began.

This is the historical background of *Flotsam* which, in many respects, is a novel that tries to document the refugee movement and the problems encountered by the emigrants from Nazi Germany. In addition, it is Remarque's own commentary on the treatment of emigrés by the Swiss authorities, who because of Switzerland's sensitive relationship to Nazi Germany, adhered to their strict laws governing immigration and work permits for foreigners.

The novel is an intertwining of two alternating stories. Remarque alternates between reporting what happened to Kern and to Steiner. This back-and-forth reporting corresponds very well to the action itself, which also goes back and forth from country to country and tends to be episodic. What actually happens is very little: Kern and Steiner, like many ancillary characters of the novel, are forced to cross and recross borders until they either die or are able to leave Europe altogether. Through all of these characters Remarque succeeds in describing what the life of exiles in 1937–38 was like.

Remarque himself did not suffer physically from being in exile. But he did encounter annoying bureaucratic difficulties with the Swiss, and also later with the American authorities when his wife Jeanne wanted to emigrate to the United States. Furthermore, when he was in the United States he was affected by the curfew laws that prevented him from leaving his home at night, just like all other "enemy aliens." He had lost his German market, and did not have the support of his German readers. He could not travel any more to or within Europe and thus lost the emotional support and integration into the society of his homeland. And so he shared his heroes' suffering in emotional respects, their experience of emotional isolation, of being cut off from their accustomed environment.

It is also clear that the title of the American edition, *Flotsam*, does more justice to the content of the novel than the German title, *Liebe deinen Nächsten*, which translates into the Christian commandment "Love thy neighbor." Although there were many people who helped the refugees from Nazi Germany in other countries, the German title implies a bitterness about the lack of love and understanding these countries had for the refugees. Remarque is very careful, however, not to present only negative representatives of the countries that took in refugees. He thus describes Kern receiving a temporary residence permit in Czechoslovakia. In Switzerland Kern meets a police officer who gives him the opportunity to escape when he is denounced by Ammers. He meets a judge who shows a lot of understanding although he cannot do anything for Kern because his hands are tied by the law. In Paris the police often look the other way and permit the emigrés to work for a while for the World Exhibition; they do not regularly raid the refugee hotels. To be sure, there are a lot of negative characters and experiences described as well: the Austrian policeman who beats

Steiner; the people who yell "slaughter those refugees!" (F 8); the Jew Oppenheim, who safely lives in Switzerland and defends Nazi Germany, unwilling to believe the reports from there; the thief who steals Kern's money after posing as a former concentration camp inmate.

The refugees have been innocently forced into their situation because of their racial or political background in the same manner as the recruits of World War I. Their overriding concern is, just as in Remarque's war novels, their physical and/or mental survival. In these novels the exile situation has assumed the function of war in the previous novels. The individual is threatened by hunger, physical abuse in the form of police brutality, unemployment, and an indifferent or often harassing bureaucracy. Their dream is always to obtain the legitimacy which passports, visas, and identification cards would give them. Their formal education is of no value any more; all that counts now is their practical ability to survive. Thus the student Kern meets his old professor in Prague and advises him not to sell vacuum cleaners or insurance policies, but small items everyone can use. It was the older, more experienced soldiers, the Katczinskys, who were able to survive during the war, and here too the more experienced refugees such as Steiner turn out to be the most resilient and resourceful ones, who take newcomers like Kern under their wings and teach them the art of survival. Steiner's intelligence and wit assume almost picaresque characteristics when he takes revenge for Ammers's having Kern arrested: he pretends to be a Nazi official visiting party members abroad and is able to extort a substantial contribution for supposed Nazi activities from Ammers. The didactic aspect of this scene is also important as a narrative device insofar as it affords Remarque the opportunity to tell his readers what it takes to survive as a refugee.

By moving the action of his novel from Vienna through Prague and Zurich to Paris, Remarque demonstrates what the prevailing xenophobic conditions in each of these neighboring countries were like for the refugees. We become familiar with the individual attitudes of the people and the behavior of the officials, policemen, and judges. We learn about the regulations and laws, the possibilities for refugees to earn a living, to obtain counterfeit passports or identification cards, the strict border and hotel controls, and the various penalties for illegal residence. *Flotsam* may thus be called a repository of exile lore.[1]

Flotsam is a colorful novel, not so much because of its action, which consists of the constant border crossings of its protagonists, but because of the great number of vivid characters and their various lives. Coincidental meetings play too much of a role to be convincing. For example, Kern asks for perfume in a store in Prague where his own father previously tried to sell the formula for his perfume. Time and again he meets a refugee whose dream is to eat a fried chicken and who is usually arrested before he is able to do so. Other characters such as a modern wandering Jew, Father Moritz, and the former member of the German parliament, Marill, continuously meet each other. Kern and Ruth manage to get a visa to go to Mexico, and Steiner leaves them enough money in his will for the passage on the steamship. Finally, Steiner takes revenge on his enemy Steinbrenner and kills him, himself committing suicide in the process but at least also escaping any further torture.

The novel is very sentimental, the most extreme example of this sentimentality being the story of the streetwise Binding, who advises Kern on how to survive as a refugee in Switzerland. Binding does not, however, have the courage to tell his mother that her other, favorite son has committed suicide. He has written her many letters in his brother's name. The story about the Catholic refugee whose son has denounced him is a cliché, as is the story about a Russian emigré who helps Steiner get his Austrian passport. The Jewish pawnbroker from whom Kern buys back Ruth's mother's ring is also stereotypical, as is the story of the former officer whose best soldier was a Jew and who now pays the restaurant bill for Kern and Ruth Holland. It seems that at times Remarque's imagination plays tricks on him and that he is more interested in arriving at a cleverly constructed and surprising conclusion or describing colorful and likable characters than in verisimilitude. But there are other parts of the novel that are very well written and portray colorfully described characters. One of the best stories has to do with the formerly successful lawyer Goldbach, whose wife left him and who then mechanically cuts to pieces the neckties he was previously trying to peddle. Another great story is the one about the former actress who allows a downtrodden man to spend the night with her before she commits suicide. It is amazing that Remarque is able to describe this scene without becoming melodramatic.

Marxist critics have pointed out that *Flotsam*, with the killing of Steinbrenner by Steiner, signals a kind of political awakening on Remarque's part.[2] Steinbrenner's murder would then be an antifascist act. This is, however, not borne out by the text. First, Steiner's antifascist attitude is not any stronger than any other refugee's in the novel. Second, his anti-Nazi activities prior to the beginning of the novel have in no way moved him to join the organized antifascist resistance abroad. Third, Steiner knew very well that going back to Germany to see his dying wife would mean that in all probability he would be apprehended and killed by the Nazis. Thus, killing Steinbrenner in the process of killing himself was rather an accidental act of personal revenge and defense than an act of general political resistance. Steiner had returned to Germany to be with his dying wife and not to fight against National Socialism and its representatives. The same applies in Remarque's next novel, *Arch of Triumph*, where his hero Ravic kills his former torturer. Although both acts can be interpreted as the self-defense of the individual against fascism, out of revenge or out of a moral and ethical outrage, they are not conscious political acts of resistance. When in *Flotsam* the former member of parliament, Marill, talks to the Communist Waser, he rejects the "revolutionary enlightenment of the masses" (F 399), rejects things political and thus the participation in any leftist movement. In short, although Remarque again uses a concrete political and historical background for his novel, and although the fate of his protagonists is determined by the political events of the time, he concentrates on their individual fate and does not relinquish a reticent attitude in political matters. The substance of the novel is rather a concern about other human beings, and in this sense the German title may be taken at face value as Remarque's own statement: *Liebe deinen Nächsten* (Love thy neighbor).

In spite of its timely theme the book was not well received in the United States. It may be considered the low point of Remarque's career in this country. Although it garnered universal respect for the refugee theme, its melodramatic execution and episodic structure failed to marshal universal approval.

Arch of Triumph (Arc de Triomphe)

The survival of refugees from the Third Reich is the theme continued in Remarque's next novel, *Arch of Triumph*, his second best-seller, particularly in America where it was first published. It was translated into at least fifteen languages, and a total of four to five million copies were printed. Over two million copies were sold in the United States alone. The novel was first serialized in *Collier's* magazine from September 15 to October 20, 1945, and the book appeared in the beginning of the new year, 1946. Remarque again had a better sense for what the public wanted to read than his publishers; when he presented the novel to his American publisher, Little, Brown, he got a rather skeptical reaction. Who, after the end of the war, would still want to read about exile and Hitler Germany? The first American edition of the novel was then published by Appleton-Century. It stayed for months on the American best-seller list—although the theme, the plot, and their professional if not to say slick execution accounted not only for its great commercial success but also for the disenchantment of many American reviewers.

As opposed to *Flotsam* this novel has only one protagonist, an exile called Ravic, whose real name is Ludwig Fresenburg. He is the former head surgeon of a large hospital in Germany who has been living in Paris for the past two years. In Paris Ravic works as a "ghost" surgeon for the less skilled French doctor Veber and the aging fashionable doctor Durant. He lives in the Hotel International, a refugee hotel populated by German, German Jewish, Spanish, and Russian refugees. The hotel guests include Ravic's friends Boris Morosow, a refugee from the Russian Revolution who now works as a doorman at the Russian nightclub Scheherazade.

One night Ravic meets a beautiful and capricious woman, Joan Madou, outside on the street. Their relationship soon becomes a bittersweet and, due to her unpredictable character, a problem-ridden love affair. Ravic is arrested by the French police when he gives first aid to a woman in the street and is consequently deported to Switzerland. When he returns several months later, Joan is living with another man, an actor, who later shoots her in a fit of jealousy. The bullet is lodged in her neck and cannot be easily removed. Ravic's skill as a surgeon turns out to be useless when it is most important to him. After Joan and Ravic have said their good-byes to each other and declared their love, Ravic gives her a lethal injection to end her suffering.

Parallel to this love story is the description of Nazi terror and revenge. Back in Germany in 1933 Ravic had helped two friends escape the Gestapo. He and his beautiful girlfriend, Sybil, were questioned and tortured by a Gestapo officer by the name of Haake. Ravic was sent to a concentration camp but managed to escape from the camp's hospital. Now in Paris, Ravic meets Haake again and, unrecognized, befriends him. Ravic gets his opportunity for revenge when they meet again several weeks later. He pretends to take Haake for a supposed pleasurable evening to a nonexistent house of assignation in the woods. Ravic kills him on the way.

By killing Haake, Ravic is able to come to terms with his past, after the encounter with Joan woke him from his lethargy and made him love life again. When France declares war on Germany at the end of the novel, Ravic allows himself to be arrested and taken to a French internment camp. He has found inner peace and simply wants to survive the war.

The time the story of *Arch of Triumph* takes place can be historically pinpointed: at the beginning of the novel a gigantic blue-white-red (French) flag has been raised in Paris for the twentieth anniversary of the armistice, which means that the current date must be November 11, 1938. At the end of the novel France declares war on Germany, therefore it must be September 3, 1939. Moreover, before she dies, Joan talks about a year having passed since she first met Ravic. During this year before the outbreak of the war many things have happened in the political arena which are referred to or at least mentioned in passing in the novel. Ravic's rich friend, Kate Hegstroem, talks about her former husband having turned from a charming good-for-nothing into a screaming Storm Troop leader. This most likely occurred around the time when Hitler's troops marched into Austria, March 11, 1938, and were enthusiastically received by the Austrians, particularly the Austrian Nazis. On September 29, 1938, the Munich Conference took place, which is referred to several times in the novel. Hitler, Mussolini, Daladier, and Chamberlain participated in this conference, which dealt primarily with Hitler's claim to those areas of Czechoslovakia that were predominantly inhabited by Germans and that, Hitler insisted, should be reunited with Germany. Later, the Pact of Munich was often referred to as the most questionable example of the great powers' appeasement policy; when Chamberlain returned to England, he spoke the famous words: "Peace in our time," not realizing how wrong he was and that he had helped encourage Hitler to make further demands. On November 9, 1938, the first great attack on Jewish businesses and synagogues in Germany occurred. On March 15, 1939, German troops marched into Czechoslovakia which was transformed into the Protectorate Bohemia and Moravia. Germany attacked Poland on September 1, 1939, and France and England were forced to declare war. Within days German nationals, throughout France, were arrested and put in internment camps.

This historical background is important to understanding the novel, especially with regard to Ravic's personal situation. All the historical facts mentioned above are alluded to in the novel. However, except for the final internment, they do not per se affect Ravic's life. His situation is static; he is an exile who has fled from Nazi Germany to France, does not have a residence or working permit, and therefore must always be concerned about police raids. Since he is not registered, he cannot rent an apartment but must stay in one of the dubious hotels for exiles that do not always report their guests to the police. If he is caught, he faces the same fate as Steiner and Kerner in *Flotsam*, deportation, most likely to Switzerland, and, if caught again, he faces imprisonment. Yet in contrast to many of the other refugees in the novel Ravic is not threatened by starvation. Although his skills as a surgeon are exploited by his French colleagues, he is able to make a fairly good living, which even allows him to spend some time with Joan on the French Riviera.

Ravic's suffering is not so much physical as emotional, a suffering caused by his lethargic, negative attitude toward life. The reason for it lies not only in the fact that he had to flee from Germany, but also in the fact that he is a member of the "lost generation" of former soldiers. Katczinsky from *All Quiet on the Western Front* is even mentioned as one of the people whom Ravic/Fresenburg knew. Here, in the exile novels, the foreign environment that rejects the exiles has taken the place of the Weimar Republic in *The Road Back* and *Three Comrades*, where the World War I soldiers were also not accepted by the old society. The nurse Eugénie in Veber's clinic, who is hostile to Ravic, says early in the novel: "Mr. Ravic is a lost man. He will never build a home for himself. . . . There is no longer anything sacred to Mr. Ravic" (AT 39). In Ravic's mind man is a helpless carcass, a toy in the hands of God. "Someone experiments with us," he says to Morosow at one time, "but he doesn't seem to have found the solution as yet. We won't complain. Experimental animals too should have professional pride" (AT 263). It is thus a world without guidance or control which Ravic envisions himself in, a world view similar to that of Robby, the protagonist of *Three Comrades*.

Thus, in contrast to *Flotsam* the content of *Arch of Triumph* is not so much the life and the troubles of the exiles as it is two personal problems: first, Ravic has to come to terms with his lethargic attitude toward life; second, he has to come to terms with what has been done to him by the Nazi regime, particularly by the sadistic Gestapo officer Haake. The first problem is solved by his relation to Joan, one of the most sophisticated female characters Remarque ever created. She is no longer a kind of female "buddy" character, an almost bodiless creature like Pat in *Three Comrades*. Nor is she a girl like Ruth, who for the first time encounters real love in her relationship with Kern. Rather, she is an experienced woman whose character combines an immense capacity for loving and at the same time a voracious lust for life. In many respects she embodies life itself. She is torn between her attraction to Ravic, whom she does really love, and her lust for life. She is not logical, but playful and uncontrollable, so that her off-and-on relationship with Ravic develops into a battle of the sexes. The dialogues with Ravic are without a doubt among the most realistic and powerful ones

Remarque ever wrote, particularly when he also blends in Ravic's interpretive thoughts during these conversations or when both talk without addressing or understanding each other. It is a most convincing rhetorical device when just before Joan's death Ravic and Joan talk to each other in the language of their childhood: Joan speaks Italian and Ravic speaks German. Their inner feeling of togetherness is so complete that it can only be expressed in their most personal language. Whether or not any actual communication in their respective languages takes place does not matter any more in view of the intense level of emotional communication that has been achieved.

There has been much speculation about the possible model for Joan, and it is possible that Marlene Dietrich may have been the woman Remarque had in mind, particularly since he spent time with her in Paris immediately preceding the outbreak of World War II. The description of Joan given on the first page of the novel fits Marlene Dietrich: "He [Ravic] saw a pale face, high cheekbones and wide-set eyes. The face was rigid and mask-like." Similarly, it has been suggested that there is a lot of Remarque himself in the character of Ravic in his outlook on life at this time, a man who has mastered the skills of surviving as an exile, "while at the same time remaining faithful to his innate sense of decency and human dignity."[3]

Such possible identities are, however, of little consequence for the understanding of the novel. The fact is that Ravic is desolate and experiences aspects of his own personality that he had never known before. Ravic finds himself and is awakened to an affirmation of life again, a kind of vitalistic enthusiasm for life, by Joan. Remarque seems to be saying that love provides the only inner stronghold for his character who seemed to have previously yielded to hopelessness and desolation. *Arch of Triumph* then is primarily a dramatic love story set against the background of Paris during the last year before the beginning of World War II.

Second, it is a novel of revenge for the cruelty and injustice committed by the Nazi regime. Haake as the representative of Hitler Germany is a stereotypical character who has a lot in common with Steinbrenner in *Flotsam*. However, whereas Steiner only accidentally takes revenge because he is caught when he returns home to his dying wife, Ravic takes revenge intentionally by seeking out Haake and managing to kill him in a perfect murder, without leaving a trace and without being hurt or caught himself.

Marxist critics have argued that in describing Ravic's revenge as a very personal, private one, Remarque has failed as a novelist. As an exile Ravic should have made contact with the communist antifascist resistance in

France. It has even been argued that after taking revenge on Haake, Ravic might possibly be ready to join the organized resistance against the Third Reich and that this could possibly "save" him as a character. Such argumentation, however, entirely misses the point of the novel: Remarque is not interested in any form of organized resistance or political awakening, particularly not in communist terms. He is merely describing the personal struggle of his hero, his coming to terms with his own feelings and his past. To be sure, Ravic knows that he has also contributed to the fight against Nazi terror when he realizes that by killing Haake there will be one less who will torture innocent people. The murder also teaches him something about himself; namely, that he is capable of murder and could kill a stranger who actually did not matter to him.[4] But the reason for his revenge was primarily a personal one, a getting even for what Haake had done to him and to the woman he was living with in Germany at the time. Similarly, Ravic had helped his persecuted friend escape from the Nazis not because the two were against the regime, but because he personally owed him his life. The killing of Haake, then, above all serves the purpose of getting even, or getting all the bitterness from the past out of Ravic's system, to set him free, and that is indeed what it accomplishes.

Ravic has experienced love in his life, and he feels purged by settling accounts with his adversary. Consequently he is now free, and can face with a certain equanimity whatever happens politically or personally to him. Having reached this stage of maturity also confirms that he has undergone an inner development; he is one of the few Remarque heroes whose character is fully developed within the course of a novel.

The theme of exile from the Third Reich has its parallel in other kinds of exile in the novel, the prime example being the story of the Russian Morosow, one of the few Russian exiles who does not claim to have served in the czar's guard or to come from a rich aristocratic Russian family. He is older and in some respects appears even more survival-wise than Ravic, but Ravic surpasses him with respect to getting even with his enemy in the course of the novel. Since 1917 Morosow has been waiting to meet his father's killers again, but the wait and the hope have so far proven in vain. Ravic and Morosow are chess and drinking partners. Other exiles who live in the Hotel International include a group of Spaniards, old royalists and partisans of the dictator Primo de Rivera who, after General Francisco Franco's victory in the Spanish Civil War, are not able to return home. The owner of the hotel changes the pictures in their rooms because their defeated enemies on the "red" Republican side are expected to arrive soon.

Remarque has skillfully introduced this farcical scene by telling us that Ravic had served as a doctor in the Spanish Civil War on the Republican side.

There are, to be sure, several sentimental scenes in the novel, notably in connection with the poor boy whose leg has to be amputated after being in a car accident and who because of the higher insurance settlement, is happy about it. There are lots of clichés, for example the good whores who have a farewell party for one of their group who plans to change her ways and reenter a more respectable bourgeois life, reminding us of a similar scene in *Three Comrades.* One may argue that the love between Ravic and Joan, particularly Joan's existence, her life with the actor, and her dramatic verbal fights with Ravic, have somewhat of a melodramatic touch. But Remarque manages skillfully to undercut such melodrama by having Ravic himself on several occasions refer to the scenes as melodramatic, as being scenes from a bad movie (AT 377, 438, 441).

The novel gains much of its momentum and suspense from the historical background and the reader's knowledge that with the outbreak of World War II, the time of the refugees in Paris is soon coming to an end. Ravic too has this knowledge and expectation. In contrast to the naïve Frenchman Veber, who stands for the majority of the French bourgeoisie, Ravic knows that Germany is not going to be appeased with minor territorial concessions and that Nazi Germany's economic policies alone are a clear indication that it will ultimately go to war. Knowing Hitler's determination and the military and organizational efficiency of the dictatorial system and its willingness to act, he cannot calm himself by relying on the French Maginot line of fortifications. Remarque is thus writing about a last year of life lived to its fullest before the great darkness falls over Europe. He writes about the packed restaurants and cafés and even the crowded brothels, and when Ravic takes Joan on a vacation trip to Nice, life there is characterized as "a brief dance of moths and gnats around the last light" (AT 203). Thus, everything is coming to an end: Joan dies, Haake is killed, Ravic interned, and darkness settles on Paris.

It is not a coincidence that the Arch of Triumph in the center of Paris and thus of France was chosen as the symbolic title of the book. At the end of the novel the arch stands in the darkness of Paris, symbolizing the darkness of suffering and war, a darkness that is descending over all of Europe: "The car drove along the Avenue Wagram and turned into the Place de l'Etoile. There was no light anywhere. The square was nothing but darkness. It was so dark that one could not even see the Arc de Triomphe" (AT 455).

NOTES

1. Harley U. Taylor, Jr., *Erich Maria Remarque* (New York: Peter Lang, 1989) 148.
2. E. g. Alfred Antkowiak, *Erich Maria Remarque* (Berlin: Volk und Wissen, 1980) 76.
3. Taylor 171.
4. Richard Arthur Firda, *Erich Maria Remarque* (New York: Peter Lang, 1988) 135.

CHAPTER FOUR

Inside the Third Reich

Spark of Life (Der Funke Leben)

No environment or historical time lends itself more readily to the theme of the survival of the individual under the most adverse historical and social conditions than the years of the Third Reich. This theme is predominant in all of Remarque's novels; thus he made the Third Reich or, more specifically, Nazi totalitarianism the background of two of his novels, *Spark of Life* (1952) and *A Time to Love and a Time to Die* (1954). By doing so he gave his readers a picture of life under the Nazi dictatorship.

Since he himself survived Nazi Germany as an exile in the United States, it is in these two novels that he first deviates from the basic premise of all his other novels. Here Remarque does not write about something that in one way or another he himself had personally experienced. Instead, in order to write these two novels it was necessary for him to interview people who had either experienced the Third Reich or, as in the case of *Spark of Life*, were survivors of Nazi concentration camps. Remarque also had to study written accounts of what life was like under the conditions he wanted to describe. As a result, it took him a total of five years to write *Spark of Life*, a novel describing life in a German concentration camp. It was a very difficult subject for Remarque, and he knew very well that the resulting book would be highly controversial, particularly to the German public. Most Germans did not wish to hear about or acknowledge the atrocities committed by their fellow countrymen. They wanted to forget the past and live in the present, happy to have survived the Nazi era themselves. For these reasons Remarque had trouble getting the German edition published. In the dedication found in the Library of Congress manuscript copy only, he makes the following statement:

The biggest Swiss publishing houses which had made a contract for *Spark of Life* refused to print the book after it was delivered and gave as a reason that the book and all other books of the publisher would be boycotted in Germany if it appeared. Other publishers wanted changes. When the book finally came out in Germany the reaction was to a large part hostile, guarded and resentful—to a smaller part the book was received without objections.[1]

The subject was considered likely to become too melodramatic and was tackled by comparatively few writers—among them the most well known were Alexander Solzhenitsyn, André Malraux, and Arthur Koestler. Remarque recognized this problem. But in addressing this topic he did not wish to write a documentary type of work, as did later authors such as Rolf Hochhuth (*Der Stellvertreter* [*The Deputy*, 1963]) and Peter Weiss (*Die Ermittlung* [*The Investigation*, 1965]). Instead, he felt that as a novelist he should write a work of fiction. In his dedication, Remarque justifies this choice:

> To write a documentary about concentration camps was not intended—although every detail of the story is documented. This was necessary and—alas—material for it existed in overwhelming masses—there were photographs, films, books, diaries and thousands of witnesses to interview.[2]

In *Spark of Life* Remarque tells the story of a group of inmates of a concentration camp located outside a fictitious city called Mellern. The camp he describes is not an extermination camp but a labor camp. In the story Remarque focuses on the fate of "Skeleton 509," a former journalist by the name of Koller. Under torture Koller refused to divulge the names of persons sought by the Gestapo, and so he was sent to the camp. The younger Josef Bucher was sent to the camp only because his father was the editor of a Social Democratic newspaper. Ephraim Berger, a former doctor of medicine, works in the crematorium. Old Ahasver is a seventy-two-year-old survivor of many camps, and Leo Lebenthal is a businessman who uses his business sense to secure extra food for the group. Karel is an eleven-year-old Czech boy whose parents were killed in the gas chambers.

These inmates are all political prisoners, and are already too weak for forced labor. They are allowed to spend their days in a Small Camp unit called the Mercy Division, an enclosed area where those inmates are imprisoned who are too weak to work. Most of them usually die within a few weeks. However, 509 and his friends still have the will to survive. When the city of Mellern is bombed and the end seems near, a spark of life flares up within them. The SS guards seem more lenient as the inmates' will to survive becomes stronger: Bucher and 509 are not killed after they have refused to "volunteer" for the medical experiments of Surgeon Major

Wiese. Instead, they establish contact with the communist underground movement of the camp, hide endangered inmates from the main camp, and later even obtain weapons. When the SS set the barracks on fire and shoot the prisoners who try to escape from the flames, the group fights back. Koller, although fatally wounded, manages to kill Anton Weber, the sadistic SS camp leader. In the last, symbolic confrontation Koller looks his torturer in the eye and then dies, victorious over his enemy. Finally the American tanks arrive, and the camp is liberated. The survivors are properly cared for and set free.

Parallel to this story that takes place inside the concentration camp Remarque tells the story of the psychological development of the camp commander. This *Obersturmbannführer* (lieutenant colonel), Bruno Neubauer, was formerly a low-ranked public servant who joined the Nazi party because of an obsession with personal success. Neubauer had in the past bought up property from people persecuted by the Nazi regime and had financially gained from these endeavors. Now he hides behind orders and ridiculous last-minute cosmetic changes in the camp, hoping that this will make his record look better when the Americans liberate the camp.

Although Osnabrück did not have a concentration camp, it is obvious that Remarque modeled the city of Mellern after his hometown. Mellern is an exact replica of Osnabrück, down to the street names and city layout. Although Remarque indeed did not live in Germany during the Third Reich and escaped persecution, his younger sister, Elfriede Scholz, may well have suffered for him. Thus the first American edition includes the dedication "To the memory of my sister Elfriede," a dedication also included in recent German editions. There is no character or situation in the novel that relates directly to Elfriede or her fate, but at one point Remarque sarcastically states that "one of the first cultural achievements of the Nazis had been to abolish the guillotine and reintroduce the hatchet instead" (SL 187), an obvious reference to his sister. There is one scene in which Remarque alludes to the persecution of anyone who makes the slightest defeatist remark. When Neubauer's wife urges him to leave Mellern, he is afraid that his conversation might be overheard by the maid: "Take care, for God's sake! Where's the maid? If anyone hears you, we're lost. The People's Court knows no mercy. One denunciation is enough" (SL 274–75). Remarque was well aware of the fact that by killing his sister Elfriede, the Nazis demonstrated that they actually intended to murder him.[3]

Historically speaking, *Spark of Life* contains an accurate account of the practices and typical behavior documented from a number of actual German concentration camps. The history of such camps will help the reader to better understand the novel. German concentration camps were modeled on internment camps first built by the Spanish during the 1895 revolution in Cuba and by the British in the South African Boer War. Other historical models include the Soviet forced labor camps which continued the czarist prison system after the 1917 Russian Revolution. The first Nazi concentration camps were established immediately following the burning of the German *Reichstag* (Parliament) building in the spring of 1933, soon after the Nazis' takeover. Originally part of a kind of unorganized Storm Trooper terror in 1933 and 1934, they were soon controlled by the SS administration, who perfected the system for the annihilation of their political enemies. After the Decree for the Protection of People and State (February 28, 1933), Communist and Social Democrat politicians as well as other opponents of National Socialism were randomly arrested and taken into "protective" custody to protect them from the "justified outrage" of the German people. Factory buildings and remote army barracks served as the first detention camps, which were dissolved after the SS took over the remaining camps in 1934. Special SS units, called *Totenkopfverbände* (Skull Units) were housed in barracks next to the camps and controlled the running of the camps. The most infamous German camps were Dachau, Sachsenhausen (formerly Oranienburg), Buchenwald (near Weimar), and after the annexation of Austria, Mauthausen (near Linz). The number of concentration camps increased tremendously with the occupation of Europe as now many more people from all occupied countries were sent to these camps.

Concentration camp inmates included political and philosophical enemies of National Socialism, members of former political parties and other organizations in Germany who had fought against National Socialism, cultural and community leaders who were not members of political parties, Protestant ministers and Catholic priests, and any other persons who were considered enemies of National Socialism (comp. SL 132). In addition, professional criminals, homosexuals—anyone who was considered asocial—were sent to the camps. Inmates died from hard labor, hunger, diseases, harsh punishments, and sadistic torture. Some camps had special barracks in which SS doctors conducted nonprofessional medical experiments. Beginning in 1941–42 extermination camps, the most horrifying invention of the Third Reich, were established in Poland. Millions of Jews from Germany and occupied areas were transported to these camps, where they were executed in the gas chambers. The German public never knew the full extent of the cruelties committed there until much later.

Revolts and rebellions are recorded at only a very few concentration camps: Treblinka, Sobridor, and Auschwitz. Thus, Remarque does not describe a typical experience. However, he does describe an important experience which includes the theme of survival and the increasing resistance of a small group of prisoners.

In the first few pages of the novel the reader is introduced to 509 and the living conditions of the Small Camp. Remarque uses grotesque contrasts when describing the cruelties committed by the SS: "Buchsbaum, as a matter of fact [had been] not quite complete: three fingers, seventeen teeth, the toenails and a part of his genitals had been missing. He had lost them while being educated to become a useful human being. The subject of the genitals had provoked much laughter at the cultural evenings in the SS quarters" (SL 3). Traditional values such as being "educated to become a useful human being" and having "cultural evenings" are juxtaposed to the perversion of these values. Thus, Remarque underlines National Socialism as an inhuman and relentless force. Although he points out that 509 and his friends have been reduced to nothing but their pure, naked existence, he hastens to confirm that there is a reason for them to go on living. This will to survive is considered "a desperate remnant of resistance" (SL 12). This spark of life grows into ever clearer resistance in the novel and is the impetus for the development of the plot. The increasing inner resistance is equivalent to becoming "a human being again—a beginning" (SL 65). When the city of Mellern is bombed by Allied aircraft for the first time, the veterans of the Small Camp are hopeful because they now see the system as not entirely indestructible. They slowly notice that the strict discipline of the camp is falling apart and that the SS guards are becoming weaker, concerned only about their personal futures.

The most conclusive evidence that things are changing in the camp is that Bucher and Koller are not killed when they refuse to volunteer for Surgeon Major Wiese's scientific experiments. That their survival is only a result of Neubauer's personal dislike for the surgeon is of little significance. The prisoners now believe that there may be a chance for survival, and they realize that some must survive in order to stand as witnesses. One telling example of this consciousness change is that 509, previously reduced only to a number, suddenly remembers his own name, Friedrich Koller. Thus he regains his individuality as a human being.

Remarque's indebtedness to vitalism is more prominent here than anywhere else in his oeuvre. Not only are individuals fighting back in this novel, but life itself begins to rebel against extinction. Life triumphs over all extremes and against all odds. As in his earlier novels Remarque paints pictures of a flourishing nature, of springtime and lush growth, at the end of his novel, signifying hope and future. When at the very end Bucher and his girlfriend, Ruth Holland, leave the camp together, they see nature, grass, leaves, and flowers, and Bucher experiences "the feeling that one is alive. . . . Simply that one lives" (SL 363). The final pages of the novel describe the survival of Bucher and Ruth Holland as they leave the camp to start a new life—one of the few works by Remarque with an optimistic ending. In contrast to the love affairs he described in *Three Comrades* and *Arch of Triumph*, here there is hope. Their love will triumph over all of their terrible experiences. Even Koller's death does not shroud this positive outlook, because he had won a physical and moral victory over his torturer, Weber. Bucher's and Ruth Holland's love remains the final statement in the novel.

The principal theme in the novel is not merely an impersonal love of life or the survival of life against all odds, but a personal humanism, a proclamation of man as the ultimate value, of human beings free from any ideologies, whether National Socialist or Communist. In his dedication Remarque states that the "dignity of man . . . cannot be destroyed by any (one person) from outside—only by himself."[4] And when 509, who obviously serves as Remarque's mouthpiece in this novel, is asked whether he is a Communist or a Social Democrat, he replies: "Just a human being—if that satisfies you" (SL 127). Before his arrest the journalist Koller had fought the Nazis and the Communists "for humaneness, tolerance and the right of the individual" (SL 280). These are clearly the values Remarque advocates here. But 509/Koller is not only Remarque's mouthpiece in the text but also the representative of the German middle class that adhered to traditional, idealistic human values without identifying with any of the political parties of the right or the left. Historically this political nonalliance may have decisively contributed to the Nazis' political success, but this does not diminish the validity of the traditional values which Remarque and many other Germans believed in.

Remarque confirms the fact that the Communists had the best underground organizations in the camps and that perhaps their organizations made up the most effective resistance movement within the Third Reich. In the Mellern concentration camp the Communists carefully prepare an uprising and plan to take over power once the SS leave. Koller cooperates with the Communists only because of the resistance organization, not for ideological reasons. It is clear that he does not want to join their ranks ideologically and he does not want to cooperate with them after the war. He considers a discussion with a Communist just as pointless as one with a Nazi. However, Koller does talk to the Communist Werner, whom he has known from before his internment. Werner admits that his party would also resort to killing, torturing, and concentration camps, not out of cruelty but out of necessity. The idea of something being necessary purely for party purposes is also totalitarian, according to Remarque/Koller. In response to the word necessity Koller replies: "I have heard that often enough. That's what Weber explained to me when he stuck lighted matches under my fingernails. It was necessary in order to extract information" (SL 292). In Remarque's opinion Communism is just another totalitarian ideology, and in *Spark of Life* he makes that even clearer than in *Arch of Triumph*. This is, of course, contrary to how Marxist critics see Remarque. For them he represents a Cold Warrior who has fallen victim to the badmouthing of Communism by the imperialist reaction.[5] Without a doubt *Spark of Life* contains Remarque's strongest attack on Nazi totalitarianism as well as totalitarian Communism. Clearer than in any other novel Remarque reveals himself as a pacifist, showing his distrust of any party affiliations.

As Alfred Antkowiak rightfully points out, Koller is not a cynical, weak hero who does not know what to live for.[6] Koller's situation is similar to Bäumer's in *All Quiet on the Western Front*; he also is part of a small group of friends trying to survive. However, as opposed to *All Quiet on the Western Front*, their enemy is not the abstract notion of death represented by an anonymous war. They have concrete enemies; National Socialism as a concrete ideology and SS men: Weber, Neubauer, and their representatives among the criminal inmates who are heading the individual barracks. Koller does not suffer from a lack of direction he can blame on the war or a feeling of a lost youth as Bäumer does. Koller knows exactly who he is and what he wants; he wants to survive. Like Ravic in *Arch of Triumph* he undergoes a personal development: from an anonymously vegetating and barely surviving individual to a resolute man able to resist and finally to fight back. When he finally kills his enemy, Weber, he acts not merely out of a feeling of personal revenge as Steiner and Ravic did; he acts for his friends, to save them from being killed. When he stares at the dying Weber, it is his own will to survive and resist, his own dignity and humaneness, that has proven victorious over the cruelty and contempt for human beings. Remarque is telling his reader that even under the most adverse conditions man can die with dignity and thus triumph over his enemy.

Remarque uses the fate of individual members of the group around 509 to demonstrate Nazi terror, and he presents characters such as Weber and Neubauer as typical Nazis. He explores Neubauer's inner motivations in such detail that Neubauer becomes one of the most well-rounded characters he has ever described. Whereas Weber is presented to us as a young SS man without any feelings, only deriving pleasure from torturing others, Neubauer is the proverbial small-time Nazi who joined the party in order to further his personal career and fortune. His character is a strange mixture of thoughtlessness, egotism, and lower-middle-class mentality so common to many Nazis. Hannah Arendt has termed this type of mentality the "banality of evil," the, as Firda defines it, "incredible use of mediocrity and slave-like compliance by the technocracy of the mass state."[7] Neubauer's party membership has given him, a former post office clerk, the chance to gain a position of power and influence, to enrich himself at the expense of others and become a good provider for his wife and daughter. Like many historical SS officers, such as Adolf Eichmann, the Nazi administrator in charge of the extermination camps, Neubauer is split between his activities as a concentration camp commander and his attempt to lead a normal family life in the city with his wife and daughter and a garden where he can pet his Angora rabbits. Iron discipline in the fulfillment of what he considers his duty alternates with sentimentality and his love for family and animals. He tries to hide behind the slogan "An order is an order." The Führer has said he would take the responsibility for everything. These were typical excuses Nazis used to defend themselves after 1945. Neubauer's attempts to have the inmates plant flower beds in front of the barracks and his passing out clothing and more food shortly before the arrival of the Americans cannot compensate for the atrocities committed under his command.

Remarque's fear that National Socialism will rise again years later is revealed when Weber tells Neubauer that he will go underground after the possible defeat and probably work for the police under an assumed identity: "We'll come up again—though possibly under other names. As Communists, for instance" (SL 304). Another SS guard is concerned whether or not his pension will be paid, which shows Remarque's criticism of the fact that many pensions were later paid to former Nazis. Another Nazi wants to escape via Spain to Argentina, as many in fact did. Almost all Nazis in the text do not consider themselves guilty "because they had acted under orders only and were free of any personal or human guilt" (SL 334). Such passages doubtless caused Remarque's Swiss publisher to fear the worst for the reception of the book. But it is wrong to attribute the negative reception in West Germany solely or even principally to the resentment of a German readership against a fellow German living comfortably in America. It must also be pointed out that *Spark of Life* is a concentration of clichés about everything that happened in German concentration camps and about the German character, including the camp commander Neubauer. Not only does Remarque's vitalistic outlook give the impression of being outdated, his collection of standard scenes and characters contains too many truisms. Together, they are simply not convincing and do not show Remarque at his best.

Most American reviewers did not recognize these weaknesses; rather, they defended the book against the reproach of not having been written by an eyewitness by pointing out that an eyewitness could not have done more justice to its theme: "But no actual survivor of a concentration camp has been able to draw up such a savage or eloquent indictment as has Erich Maria Remarque in *Spark of Life.*"[8] There is no doubt that the book's irrepressible confidence in the will to survive and in the power of the human spirit in the face of all moral and physical degradation, personified in a protagonist struggling to win a moral victory, was particularly appealing to American reviewers, and to the reading public as well.

A Time to Love and a Time to Die
(Zeit zu leben und Zeit zu sterben)

Both the American and the German edition of *A Time to Love and a Time to Die* appeared in the same year, 1954. The American edition appeared first. Since the English translation of the German title—Remarque always wrote in his native language—was "a time to live and a time to die," one can only assume that the English title was the result of marketing considerations.

The novel continues Remarque's treatment of life inside the Third Reich. This time he tells his story from the perspective of a German Everyman, here the soldier Ernst Graeber. Graeber is a common soldier at the Russian front during spring 1943, after the disaster of the Sixth German Army at Stalingrad, when the German troops were retreating. With the beginning of the German retreat Graeber begins thinking about National Socialism and what it has done to the German people. His doubts are reinforced when he goes back on a three-week furlough to his northern German hometown, Werden. Much of Werden, including the house his parents used to live in, has been reduced to rubble by Allied air raids. He is unable to locate his parents or even find out whether they are still alive. When he tries to visit an old family friend, Health Councilor Kruse, to inquire about his parents' whereabouts, he finds that Kruse has been sent to a concentration camp.

Graeber falls in love with Kruse's daughter Elisabeth, whom he remembers as a young schoolgirl. The only help he gets looking for his parents is from a former schoolmate, Alfons Binding, who is now an SA commander. Binding provides Graeber with food until Binding dies in an air raid. Graeber and Elisabeth get married and manage to spend a few happy weeks together. Graeber visits his former teacher, Pohlmann, who was forced to resign from teaching and is now hiding a Jew. Searching for an answer to his moral dilemma, Graeber is told by Pohlmann that every individual must make his own decision. Pohlmann is later arrested by the Gestapo. After his return to his unit at the Russian front, Graeber refuses to kill four Russians who are suspected to be partisans, instead killing the overzealous Nazi Steinbrenner. After he has allowed the Russians to flee, Graeber himself is killed by one of them with his own gun.

There are several indirect references to Remarque's sister Elfriede Scholz and her fate. One is when Remarque reports that Mrs. Lieser most likely denounced Health Councilor Kruse; another is when Mr. Loose, another friend of Graeber's family, is afraid that his wife, having gone mad over the fact that her children have been killed in an air raid, might say something critical about the Nazi regime. The most obvious reminder of Elfriede is, however, when Graeber sees a newspaper photograph of the head of the German People's Court, Freisler, the man who sentenced Remarque's sister to death. The newspaper reports that four people had been beheaded because they did not believe in the German victory any more.

The German publication of the novel caused much controversy following the discovery that there were certain differences between the English, the Danish, and the German editions. These differences were first outlined in an article in the Copenhagen newspaper *Information*, where it was charged that certain changes were deliberately made in the German edition in order not to offend German sensibilities. The German publisher, Kiepenheuer and Witsch, emphatically denied any such intention, replying: "The publishing house would never submit an author such as Erich Maria Remarque to censorship and Erich Maria Remarque, for his part, would never submit to censorship."[9] Kiepenheuer and Witsch claimed that Remarque had himself requested the publisher to check the "question of milieu, of terminology and other things relating to the external aspects of the novel." The publishers asserted that they had carefully read the manuscript to check for inaccuracies as requested by Remarque. The proposed changes were then submitted to Remarque and were approved by him.

There can be no doubt, however, that the changes and omissions in the German edition were made intentionally to diminish the possible negative impact of the novel on the German reading public. The main changes are as follows:

1. References to Steinbrenner as being a former member of the SD, the security service of the SS, and a block warden in a concentration camp are missing in the German edition.

2. Missing also are more detailed references to Steinbrenner's racist, anti-Semitic statements in connection with his planned marriage and references to his own participation in the killing of Jews.

3. Missing is the description of Steinbrenner sending Hirschland's mother a telegram falsely notifying her of her son's death. There are no references to Hirschland being half-Jewish; in the German edition there is only a soldier by the name of Hirsch*mann*.

4. Narrations by the SS man Heini about sadistic treatment and killings of prisoners in Russia were omitted.

5. Approximately one page of the discussion between Graeber and Pohlmann about collective guilt of the Germans is missing in the German edition.

Although these changes do indicate that some censorship took place, not all such references were omitted. Many other statements pointing the finger at the Germans and referring to personal responsibility were not taken out.

It is tempting to compare this novel to *All Quiet on the Western Front*. There are structural parallels: both describe war action at the beginning and the end and a visit to the hometown in the center. A similar detail is the fact that in both novels the hero is reprimanded for not properly saluting a pensioned officer at home. But that is as far as the similarities go. *A Time to Love* does not attempt to describe the atrocities of war; such references are limited to the first pages of the book, where Remarque describes different ways in which bodies decompose in the various climates of the German fronts all over Europe and in Africa. As a matter of fact, no front-line combat action is directly described in *A Time to Love and a Time to Die*. Whereas in *All Quiet on the Western Front* Paul Bäumer spends his furlough at home in an environment which, except for a lack of food, seems largely undisturbed by the war, Ernst Graeber in *A Time to Love and a Time to Die* experiences the air raids and their effects on the German civilian population. Whereas Paul Bäumer visits his parents and friends at home, Ernst Graeber is not even able to locate his parents and consequently visits his old teacher and falls in love with an old childhood friend. Whereas in *All Quiet on the Western Front* the old patriotic and nationalistic ideals are still alive and indeed flourish at home, in *A Time to Love and a Time to Die* Remarque shows the effects of the war and of Nazi rule on the minds of the country's people; he shows the emergence of a climate of distrust, fear, and denunciation. He demonstrates that the war is taking place not only at the front where soldiers are fighting, but at home, where thousands are being killed in air raids, women and children are mutilated and buried in mass graves. This, of course, did not occur in World War I.

The main difference between the two novels is in the character of the two heroes: Paul Bäumer time and again refuses to think about the war; he is afraid of the consequences of contemplating the horrors of war. He has experienced these horrors; the people at home have not, and are therefore caught in their old-fashioned patriotic ideas. He has not drawn any theoretical or practical conclusions from his realization of the horrors of war. There are almost no political discussions of any kind in *All Quiet on the Western Front*. In *A Time to Love and a Time to Die* there are several conversations and discussions about politics, about the atrocities committed by the Nazis, particularly the SS. On the very first few pages there is talk about the difference between the SS and regular army units: the regular army does not burn and shoot to death whoever they can get hold of. The group of men around Graeber consider themselves decent soldiers, not specialists in the killing of helpless civilians like the SD. When at the Russian front the German troops were forced to retreat, Ernst Graeber had already begun to think. His old mentor Fresenburg, commander of the Fourth Company, is his close friend. Their relationship is similar to that of Kern and Steiner in *Flotsam*. It is Fresenburg who opens Graeber's eyes at the front and advises him to see Pohlmann during his leave. Fresenburg tells Graeber quite clearly what is obviously Remarque's own message about the Nazi era: "We have lost our standards. For ten years we have been isolated— isolated in a hideous inhuman and ridiculous arrogance that cries to heaven. We have been proclaimed Herrenvolk [master race] whom the others have to serve as slaves. . . . Herrenvolk—to obey every charlatan, every command—what has that to do with Herrenvolk?" (TL 37–38). And he concludes: "We have broken every agreement, every human law." These seeds fall on fertile ground in Graeber's mind, so that shortly after he comes home and meets Elisabeth, he is able to conclude about life inside Nazi Germany: "drowned in lies and fear, hunted under the earth and at war with light and purity and truth" (TL 105). To be sure, he also sees that his life has been reduced to a banal existence, just like that of Paul Bäumer. But unlike Paul Bäumer, Graeber's homecoming becomes a quest for truth: "He had gone away often enough and refused to know. He and a hundred thousand others. And they had thought in that way they could quiet their consciences. He no longer wanted that. He no longer wanted to evade. He had not come back on furlough for that purpose" (TL 162). He wants to understand completely the events of the time, and that is the reason he looks up Pohlmann. In the German edition the conversation with Pohlmann is somewhat disappointing because, as previously pointed out, some important statements regarding the problem of German collective guilt were eliminated. Even so, Pohlmann is unable to give Graeber a clear-cut answer. He simply states that all his books—poems, great German literature and philosophy—do not fit together with the inhumanity of the SA, the concentration camps, and the liquidation. Both just coexist. "If the men who wrote these books were alive most of them would be sitting in a concentration camp too" (TL 249). Although he is the representative of traditional German humanist values, of the best of the educated German middle class, neither he nor his books are able to give a clear-cut answer. He just acknowledges that choices are difficult to make in such times, but no one can escape the personal responsibility of deciding for himself.

Perhaps his own actions can speak for themselves. He sets an example by teaching the truth and by hiding a Jew—being arrested for it. It is not merely a coincidence that the conversation with Pohlmann is in the center of the book and that an older mentor is teaching Graeber. Graeber decides to go back to the front as a soldier because otherwise his wife and his parents would be in danger. But in Russia he is again confronted with a decision when Steinbrenner wants to kill the Russians who are considered partisans. At home he was not quite ready to kill the SS man Heini when he was following him. But at this point he takes action and kills Steinbrenner, the representative of National Socialism, letting the Russians get away. Thus, he carries out exactly what Fresenburg had advocated: to do everything in his power to prevent all this from ever happening again. This is ultimately Remarque's own message to his readers. Thus, whereas Bäumer does not undergo any psychological development in the course of *All Quiet on the Western Front*, Graeber does. He develops and adopts new ideals, personal ideals of humanity within a society that has given up such ideals, and he develops in the direction of active resistance. That the partisans whom he freed ironically are the ones who shoot him does not negate his conversion.

There are also certain similarities to *Spark of Life*. *A Time to Love and a Time to Die* describes concentration camp inmates who are sent to the city in order to clear away the rubble left from the bombing raids. Other similarities include official representatives of the Third Reich, the SA and the SS, who again display pure inhuman cruelty (Heini) or the kind of evil and naïve Romanticism seen in Neubauer.

Graeber's friend Binding is somewhat problematic. On the one hand he sends a former teacher to a concentration camp for personal revenge. On the other hand he tries to help Graeber, who was never his close friend. As opposed to *Spark of Life* the statements equating National Socialism with Communism are much shorter. In Graebers's/Remarque's view both of these ideologies represent a totalitarian government and prevent people from thinking for themselves.

Remarque likes contrasts. In the middle of the description of the air raids he describes one of the most luxurious dinners with the best wines. Graeber is dining with Elisabeth, and Remarque carefully spares Witte's Restaurant from harm, an idyllic place where Graeber and Elisabeth enjoy happy hours together, totally removed from anything connected with the presence of Nazis or war. This supper at Witte's Restaurant seems to idealize a type of modest happiness, a Biedermeier ideal that we find in the nineteenth-century Swiss writer Gottfried Keller's *Romeo and Juliet in the Village* as well as in the novels of twentieth-century New Objectivity.

Like *Spark of Life*, *A Time to Love and a Time to Die* ends optimistically, although in both novels the hero dies. In *Spark of Life* Bucher and Ruth Holland were able to leave the concentration camp and start a new life; in *A Time to Love and a Time to Die* Elisabeth is probably expecting a baby by Graeber. This is not an accidental or unwanted pregnancy. When asked by Graeber why she wants to bring a child into such a poisoned atmosphere, one that will probably last for years even after peace has been restored, she replies: "To educate it against that. What's to happen if the people who are against everything that is happening now don't want to have children? Are only the barbarians to have them? Then who's to put the world to rights again?" (TL 338). In the very center of the novel a linden tree is presented as a symbol of life. At the end it is life itself that will prevail.

Whereas the reception of Remarque's latest work in Germany again centered around the questions of authenticity and personal involvement, American critics were largely positive, at times even comparing it favorably to *All Quiet on the Western Front*. Despite some grumbling about the "slightly glib, and at times faintly manufactured flavor,"[10] Remarque's honorable intentions of waging war against the inhumanity of ideological systems was acutely perceived.

NOTES

1. Quoted Richard Arthur Firda, *Erich Maria Remarque* (New York: Peter Lang, 1988) 147.
2. Quoted Firda 146.
3. Harley U. Taylor, Jr., *Erich Maria Remarque* (New York, Peter Lang, 1989) 194.
4. In a manuscript copy of *Spark of Life* in the Library of Congress. Quoted Firda 146.
5. Alfred Antkowiak, *Erich Maria Remarque* (Berlin: Volk und Wissen, 1980) 100–101.
6. Antkowiak 95.
7. Quoted Firda 154.
8. Quentin Reynolds in *The New York Times Book Review* Jan. 27, 1952.
9. This and the following quotations are from Taylor 205–06.
10. C. J. Rolo in *Atlantic Monthly* July 1954: 83.

CHAPTER FIVE

The Meaning of Life and Death

The Black Obelisk (Der schwarze Obelisk)

With *The Black Obelisk* (1956) Remarque takes up the theme of the Weimar Republic again. It is almost a continuation of the story of the soldiers in *All Quiet on the Western Front* and *The Road Back* and covers the time gap between these two novels and *Three Comrades*. The narrator and hero is Ludwig Bodmer, a salesman and an advertising and office manager in the Kroll brothers' tombstone business in the town of Werdenbrück. The story takes place between April and October 1923, the height of the inflation in Germany. It is a time when workers are paid twice a day and high-rollers become rich. The poor, particularly the war-disabled and old people who depend on pensions, are starving because their pension increases can in no way keep up with inflation. At the end of the novel things turn for the better; the value of the German mark is reestablished, and Bodmer leaves Werdenbrück for a job with a newspaper in Berlin.

Bodmer tells about his conversations with his old war comrade Georg Kroll, who has taken over his father's tombstone business. While Georg dreams of high society in Berlin and other European capitals, he has an affair with Lisa Watzek, the sensuous wife of the horsemeat butcher Watzek, who lives across the street. Bodmer participates in and listens to discussions with Heinrich Kroll, Georg's nationalistic brother who, like many Germans at the time, yearns for the good old days of the Second Empire. He witnesses the emergence of the National Socialist Party, of which Watzek is a member. He has an affair with Gerda Schneider, a very levelheaded traveling trapeze artist whom he loses to Eduard, the owner of the hotel Walhalla.

In addition to his position with the Kroll brothers, Bodmer has another job: He plays the organ during Catholic services in a local insane asylum. For this he receives, in addition to his minimal pay, a free meal with wine. During these meals he has the opportunity to have philosophical and religious discussions with the local priest, Bodendiek, and one of the hospital's doctors, Wernicke, a scientist. He also has a romantic relationship with one of the patients, Geneviève, a schizophrenic who sees herself as Isabelle most of the time. Her existence represents another, spiritual reality, far removed from anything concrete or "real." For Bodmer she represents a kind of original, unadulterated counterworld. In the end Geneviève is cured and becomes a normal young lady again. She has forgotten all of her encounters with Bodmer and her other selves.

Werdenbrück is a thinly veiled name for Remarque's native Osnabrück. Like Bodmer, Remarque also was employed as a tombstone salesman. Like Remarque, Bodmer was seventeen years old when he became a soldier, was wounded, although not critically, and brought to an army hospital. Bodmer is also described as being twenty-five years old in 1923. Like Remarque, he first became an elementary school teacher in an isolated village, as he had promised his sick mother before she died. Finally, Bodmer's departure for Berlin is similar to Remarque's own departure from Osnabrück when he left to become an editor for *Echo Continental* in Hannover. On August 6, 1956, Remarque wrote to his publisher: "For the publicity write-up on the dust jacket it is perhaps interesting that during the inflation I was working in a tombstone business and also was serving as an organist for some time in an insane asylum."[1] This clearly indicates that Remarque wanted to point out the autobiographical content of the book for advertising purposes.

Just as the city of Werdenbrück is obviously a thinly disguised Osnabrück, there is also no doubt that many of the characters of the novel were modeled after people Remarque knew. One example is Eduard Knobloch (in German *Knoblauch* means "garlic"), the owner of the Walhalla hotel, modeled after Eduard Petersilie (meaning "parsley" in German). Petersilie was the owner of the Hotel Germania which was destroyed in World War II and, just like Eduard Knobloch, Petersilie wrote poetry. The poet Hungermann was modeled after a local poet named Hungerland, and the priest Bodendiek was modelled after a priest named Bodensiek. As in *A Time to Love and a Time to Die,* Remarque does not slavishly stick to the exact geography of his native town or to the real people he knew. Rather, he changes and modifies the characters and thus creates a new, fictitious reality.

The historical background of the novel is more completely pictured than in any of Remarque's previous novels. It takes place from April to the beginning of October 1923, a time of economic chaos. Inflation, already bad during 1921 and 1922, has gotten out of control. Prices are rising so fast that new paper money could sometimes not be printed fast enough. The relationship of the German mark to the U.S. dollar has become the yardstick for prices, which thus increase daily. Remarque vividly describes how workers are paid on a daily basis and then run to the stores to buy what they can before the value of their money decreases. He describes the plight of the little people, particularly the war-disabled, who hold a rally to draw attention to their misery. In contrast to these descriptions Remarque shows smug profiteers in shining cars who watch the victims. He describes the artificial high-life atmosphere in the town's only bar, the Red Mill, where young black marketeers sip champagne at fantastic prices and do business in an atmosphere of artificial elegance. Time and again he points out how many were able to profit from the inflation by having nonperishable goods at their disposal or being able to buy now and pay later; for example, Georg Kroll and Bodmer eat at their former comrade Eduard's hotel, Walhalla, where they pay with meal coupons they bought a long time ago and which are now practically worthless. During these times even the tombstone the retired sergeant Knopf buys, or a mere grave site, becomes an investment. Remarque also shows how the only way for a businessman to survive during this runaway inflation is to buy now and pay later: Kroll's firm buys gravestones from the producer, Riesenfeld, by signing promissory notes and paying them later when the money is grossly devalued. The institution which profits the most from the inflation is the German Reich, as this is an easy way to retire all debts.

The novel ends just before the attempted coup in Munich (November 8/9, 1923) by Hitler and Ludendorff, the former chief of the German general staff during World War I. Remarque restricts himself to the relatively small town of Werdenbrück and its small-town characters, giving a rather humorous picture of life in a German city at that time. Occasional references are made to the emergence of the Nazi party, notably in connection with the butcher Watzek, who has become a member of the Storm Troopers. Other references to the political climate of the time include the change in the political mood from pacifism to nationalism, as seen in the character of Heinrich Kroll, and a similar shift in the outlook of veterans' organizations, like the one led by the former major Wolkenstein. The unveiling of a war memorial in a neighboring village leads to violence and political murder; a carpenter who dares to show the flag of the new and hated Weimar Republic instead of the old imperial flag is killed. Remarque points out here that the murders of the political Right were not adequately investigated by the authorities.

The reason for this historically accurate background is most likely due to the fact that Remarque conceived this novel as a political novel. Although he had become a pacifist after the experience of World War I, his novels written during the Weimar Republic were by no means political. A certain change occurred in Remarque during the Third Reich when the author had to flee Germany. Although he was rich and famous, he nevertheless lived in a foreign country, an exile separated from his homeland and his reading audience. The experience of the Third Reich, particularly the murder of his sister Elfriede, caused Remarque to depart from his neutral stance and to speak out. Even the earlier novel *Spark of Life* must be interpreted in terms of an admonishment never to forget. This political statement is even stronger in *The Black Obelisk*. Its outspoken political message is what distinguishes it from the earlier novels about the Weimar Republic, *The Road Back* and *Three Comrades*.

In this context it is important to consider the time in which Remarque wrote this novel, the years 1954–55. The *Bundeswehr*, the new armed forces of the Federal Republic of Germany, was in the process of being built up again, and many people all over the world, including Remarque, expressed concern about the reemergence of Germany as a military power. Whereas many victims of National Socialism were fighting for a modest pension, many of the former top officials, officers, and public servants were living very comfortably on theirs, and many of them still held high government offices. For this reason, Remarque added a preamble and an epilogue to his book in which he makes his own humanitarian principles, and indirectly his political convictions, very clear. The preamble and the epilogue form a frame for the novel; the preamble is included in the German edition, but unfortunately not in the American one, which contains the epilogue only. The preamble refers to the present Cold War and to the threat of the atomic bomb:

Do not scold me if I return to old times. Again the world is in the pale light of the apocalypse, the smell of blood and the dust of the last destruction have not dissipated yet and already laboratories and factories around the world are working at full speed to maintain peace by inventing weapons which are able to blow up the entire globe.—

The peace of the world! Never has there been more talk about it and less been done about it than in our time; never have there been more false prophets, never more lies, never more death, never more destruction and never more tears than in our century, the twentieth, the century of progress, of technology, of civilization, of mass culture and mass murder.—

So don't scold me for returning to the legendary years when hope was still wafted over us like a flag and when we believed in such suspect things as humanity, justice and tolerance—and also believed that *one* world war would be sufficient instruction for one generation.

The author's main purpose in writing this book is therefore not so much a nostalgic return to the town of his youth, but rather to express a clear warning that another war is imminent.

The epilogue, on the other hand, expresses the author's outrage about what happened during the Third Reich and the way West Germany was dealing with its past. Here the narrator points out that he never again saw any of the people he wrote about, and he briefly reports their fate during the Third Reich. Watzek, who had become a *Sturmführer* in the SA, found out about his wife's affair with Georg, and although he had been divorced five years earlier, he had Georg sent to a concentration camp where he died. The sculptor Kurt Bach was beaten so badly in a concentration camp that he became crippled and now fights for a meager pension. The poet Hans Hungermann became Cultural Guardian and *Obersturmbannführer* in the Nazi party, which he celebrated in glowing verses, and now he receives a generous pension as former school principal, just like all the Nazi generals and war criminals. For Heinrich Kroll this is proof of the beloved fatherland's unshakable sense of justice. Major Wolkenstein joined the party, had a distinguished career, and, after laying low for a few years after the war, is now employed by the Department of Foreign Affairs, along with many other party members.[2] Bodendiek and Wernicke kept a number of Jews hidden in the insane asylum. Bodendiek was later transferred to a small village because he became angry that his bishop accepted the title of Councilor of State from a government that praised murder as a sacred duty, and Wernicke lost his job because he refused to give lethal injections to his patients. Lisa Watzek was killed in an air raid. The city of Werdenbrück was largely destroyed; only picture postcards show its former condition. The insane asylum and the maternity hospital were the only buildings spared from damage, probably because they were located some distance outside the city. They even had to be substantially expanded.

The epilogue thus contains Remarque's criticism of the restoration period during the Adenauer years in West Germany: the victims of the Third Reich were not properly taken care of, and those who were responsible for the crimes committed were rewarded with pensions and high positions. Thus, the preamble and the epilogue contain a good part of Remarque's political criticism and the book's political message to the reader.

But the novel also contains much commentary on German history and many sarcastic remarks about the German character. Particularly in the character of Heinrich Kroll, Remarque characterizes the conservative German who wanted to annex large parts of France and Russia as late as 1917 and now complains about the injustice of the Versailles Treaty. He portrays the typical conservative who was a pacifist at the end of the war and now advocates a new strong German army. Heinrich has forgotten that the current problems in Germany are the result of the politics and the war of the Second Empire, as his brother Georg points out to him. Remarque continually makes fun of the blind German sense of obedience and lack of self-criticism, of the Germans' being sticklers for their principles and feeling superior to other nations, their obsession with military rank, and even their enthusiasm for belonging to various social clubs.

By choosing the time of the 1923 runaway inflation, Remarque has again chosen an exceptional time in German history for his story. The era has a sense of unreality which in some ways is similar to an exile existence. This economic unreality, however, expresses the atmosphere of the novel. In the first chapter Bodmer states:

> Money is an illusion; everyone knows that, but many still do not believe it. As long as this is so the inflation will go on till absolute zero is reached. Man lives seventy-five per cent by his imagination and only twenty-five per cent by fact—that is his strength and his weakness, and that is why in this witch's dance of numbers there are still winners and losers (BO 15).

Here he is only talking about inflation on the surface. In reality he is describing his own philosophy of life. In *The Black Obelisk* Remarque has returned to the old vitalistic philosophy of his youth. He argues against reason, for intuition; against materialism, for the force of life itself.

This is the philosophical notion behind all the Geneviève/Isabelle episodes which begin in Chapter 2 and are interspersed throughout the novel. Just as inflation has suspended the rules of the economic reality, Geneviève's schizophrenia has created an artificial, temporary reality for her. The mentally ill Geneviève continually asks Bodmer questions about the laws of physics which he cannot answer. He cannot prove that the grass behind you appears only when you turn around. He cannot tell what happens to the image in the mirror when the person goes away. Yet in a strange way she does not seem sick to him at all—on the contrary. He concludes: "She is not sick, I think, and yet I know that she is—but if she is sick, then all the rest of us are sicker" (BO 209). He feels that Isabelle is striving for essential answers rather than superficiality: "Beloved fearless heart, I think, untouched and aiming straight as an arrow at the essential alone, even if you do not reach it and go astray—but who does not go astray'' (BO 204). This striving for the essential is characteristic of the German Romantics. It is precisely this kind of Romantic yearning that Bodmer/Remarque sees embodied in the unreal character of Isabelle. This becomes clear later in the novel when Bodmer tells Isabelle that he loves her, although he cannot hold on to the moment. Isabelle replies with a classic Romantic image: ''Now at last you have felt it — the nameless happiness and the sadness and the dream and the double face! It is the rainbow, Rudolf, and you can walk across it, but if you have doubts you will fall!'' (BO 328). And shortly thereafter she adds: ''But it is enough to have the longing'' (BO 329). Isabelle thus represents the basic union of all opposites, the ceasing of all duality in a truly Romantic vision, although such a union can only exist outside the ''normal'' social world in a state of mental illness. When in the end Geneviève is cured, she becomes quite normal, talks only about trite, everyday things, and remembers nothing about Bodmer.

Just as Isabelle asks Bodmer all kinds of questions he cannot answer, so too does Bodmer ask other people in the novel questions they cannot answer. When questioned by Georg Kroll at the beginning of the novel about what the three most precious things in life are, he answers: ''How should I know that, Attorney General, when life itself is what I'm still searching for?'' (BO 7). And when someone in the street complains about his poor piano playing, he admits:

He is right. I cannot really play. Either at the piano or at life; never, never have I been able to. I have always been too hasty, too impatient; something always intervenes and breaks it up. But who really knows how to play, and if he does know, what good is it to him? Is the great dark less dark for that, are the unanswerable questions less inscrutable, does the pain of despair at eternal inadequacy burn less fiercely, and can life ever be explained and seized and ridden like a tamed horse or is it always a mighty sail that carries us in the storm and, when you try to seize it, sweeps us into the deep? Sometimes there is a hole in me that seems to extend to the center of earth. What could fill it? Yearning? Despair? Happiness? What happiness? Fatigue? Resignation? Death? What am I alive for? Yes, for what am I alive?'' (BO 31–32).

Bodmer's search is thus a search for the meaning of life. This theme makes *The Black Obelisk* fit directly into the tradition of the German *Bildungsroman*. The parallels to Thomas Mann's *Magic Mountain* are particularly obvious. Like Mann's guileless Hans Castorp, who enters the tuberculosis sanatorium where he meets a woman and two male teachers representing warring philosophies (Settembrini and Naphta), Ludwig Bodmer enters the insane asylum where he meets Geneviève/Isabelle and the priest Bodendiek and the scientist Wernicke, neither of whom can convince him of their approach to life. In the conversations with the self-confident Bodendiek, Remarque's criticism of the Catholic Church is quite evident. On the other hand, he characterizes Bodendiek in a very positive way, patterned after a priest he knew. What Bodmer criticizes in both Bodendiek and Wernicke is their self-confident attitude which is able to categorize and label everything. Wernicke points out to Bodmer that "all that is simple for me. . . . I'm a scientist. I don't believe in anything at all. I simply observe. Bodendiek, on the other hand, believes a priori! Between the two you flutter about in uncertainty" (BO 169). For Bodendiek as well as for Wernicke life has no secrets, everything is ordered according to categories:

> The man of faith and the man of science are sitting in the full brilliance of the ceiling light. For them the world is not a vague, quivering unrest, it is not a muttering from the depth or a lightning flash in the icy spaces of the void—they are men of faith and of science, they have sounding lines and plummets and scales and measures, each of them a different set but that does not matter, they are sure, they have names to put on everything like labels, they sleep well, they have a goal that contents them, and even horror, the black curtain in front of suicide, has a well-recognized place in their existence, it has a name, it has been classified and thereby rendered harmless (BO 104).

Consequently, the fact that Geneviève is cured in Wernicke's terms is only a questionable success in Bodmer's eyes, since it also means that she has lost the ability to see the secret meaning of the world around her. She can no longer overcome the duality of matter and idea. On the other hand, he must admit that Wernicke has been able to save her from possible horrible mental anguish and suffering. Whereas Bodmer/Remarque seems to criticize Bodendiek for always having a pat answer to every question and whereas he questions the dogmas of the Catholic Church, Bodmer does admit to Bodendiek toward the end that he has found God, although not within the prescribed confines of the Church.

But Bodmer has other mentors, too, and he also learns from his experiences in the "real" world. One of his mentors is his old war comrade and present employer, Georg Kroll, who has accepted the limitations of bourgeois life and has an affair with a very down-to-earth woman, Lisa Watzek. Georg Kroll has relegated all his higher aspirations to dreams and to fancy magazines about high society in Berlin. He does not reach for the stars but for things that are directly attainable within his surroundings. He is thus able to neatly separate his romantic yearning for high life from what is possible in this world. In Georg's view Bodmer is an adolescent who just has some growing up to do. Bodmer tries Georg's ways when he takes up with Gerda Schneider, a circus artist who performs at the Red Mill. He later criticizes himself for not being able to be satisfied with this kind of simple happiness: "What an ass have I been, I am thinking. Life itself [Gerda Schneider] is sitting here and I in my confused megalomania did not understand it!"[3] Immediately following this statement Georg comments: "We are celebrating Ludwig's confirmation. He is slowly turning into a man." Later, Bodmer does not want to accept the flowers from Lisa that were sent to her by Riesenfeld. If he had accepted them, he could have sent them to some girl. This shows that he has given up romantic wooing. Lisa tells him: "I think you are growing up" (BO 316).

This maturing process is complete when Bodmer decides to leave Werdenbrück to accept a minor position with a Berlin newspaper. Just as Geneviève/Isabelle has been cured, just as the inflation is over and one trillion marks have become one new mark, Bodmer's youth has passed and he must now face the reality of life in the big city. By having found his place as a normal, useful member of society, Bodmer has become a classical hero typical of the German *Bildungsroman*.

The German edition of *The Black Obelisk* bears the subtitle "The Story of a Belated Youth," a phrase that is missing from the American edition. This subtitle, possibly modeled after the subtitle of Hermann Hesse's novel *Demian: The Story of Emil Sinclair's Youth*, implies an ironic distance to the adolescent, immature behavior of the hero and some of his friends. Thus, the idea of lost youth, youth cut short by World War I, recurs in the novel; but in contrast to Remarque's earlier works, it is used ironically. The main theme, the quest for the meaning of life, is similarly ironic. In 1955 Remarque obviously had gained enough distance from his youth that he could see himself and his youthful opinions as adolescent world-weariness. He returns to his old vitalistic philosophy, but he does so in order to demonstrate how it is overcome by a more mature attitude toward life that leaves behind philosophical questioning of the meaning of life in favor of more practical, professional goals.

There are many characters and scenes in the novel that show an often raucous humor. There is, for example, the retired sergeant Knopf, who returns every night from his drinking bouts and urinates at the tombstone company's landmark, the obelisk. It is not until Bodmer scolds him while pretending to be the Kaiser about to demote him in rank that Knopf is cured. There is Mrs. Beckmann, a hefty lady who lives with the shoemaker Brill. Brill makes bets on her ability to pull nails out of the wall — with her buttocks. There is the coffin maker Wilke, who is afraid of ghosts and the cabaret singer Renée de la Tour, who is able to both sing in a soprano voice and give commands in the deep male voice of a drill sergeant. There are the members of the town's poetry society who organize an excursion to the local brothel to instill their lyrical poetry with blood and passion. Remarque has introduced the various members of the club in order to satirize his own early attempts at writing poetry. Finally, there are the ladies from the local brothel, including the one called the Iron Horse, a woman dressed in leather, who uses whips on her masochistic clients. She finally dies from a heart attack while fulfilling her duties. It is befitting that the black obelisk will be her tombstone.

The Black Obelisk is one of Remarque's best and most mature works. In it he was able to combine the motifs from his earlier works with his more mature distance and humor. He returned to the environment of his youth, drawing a colorful picture of life in his hometown Osnabrück at the time of the 1923 inflation, but also showing the necessary maturing process of his hero rather than bemoaning his lost youth.

Remarque's development as a writer becomes clear when one contrasts *The Black Obelisk* with *All Quiet on the Western Front*. Whereas *All Quiet on the Western Front* contains very few historical dates, the events of *The Black Obelisk* can be exactly pinpointed. Whereas *All Quiet on the Western Front* does not contain any analysis of the origin and purpose of World War I, in *The Black Obelisk* the author repeatedly analyses the causes and economic ramifications of the rampant inflation of 1923 and the rise of nationalism. Whereas *All Quiet on the Western Front* describes the state of war and its effect on a sensitive young man, *The Black Obelisk* describes the development of a young man toward a more realistic attitude. Whereas *All Quiet on the Western Front* contains numerous lyrical passages in which the theme of the lost youth is taken up and an emotional world view is expounded, in *The Black Obelisk* such views are primarily relegated to the Geneviève/Isabelle episodes and are laid to rest at the end. Whereas in *All*

Quiet on the Western Front Remarque decries the fact that the young soldiers have been cheated out of their youth, in *The Black Obelisk* his hero Bodmer succeeds in making it up, asks all the basic questions about the meaning of life young people must ask, and reaches a certain level of maturity at the end. Whereas *All Quiet on the Western Front* is all serious and sentimental, *The Black Obelisk* is full of raucous humor, and the hero's questioning is repeatedly put into perspective by creating distance through irony. This does detract from the merits of *All Quiet on the Western Front* as a war novel; it just shows that Remarque, the man, has grown since writing his first great success, both with respect to a more mature outlook on life and with respect to political consciousness.

It is a pity that, because of its philosophical probing and its political allusions which were not easy to pick up for many American readers, most American reviewers did not know what to think about the novel. Although they were able to appreciate its raucous, picaresque aspects, they missed the fact that Remarque also wanted to write a political novel about the Weimar Republic and its road toward Hitler's fascism. This can only in part be accounted for by the fact that the preamble is missing in the American edition. Rather, the expectations raised by the previous Remarque books prevented the reviewers from seeing this novel as revealing a different kind of Remarque: one who commingles philosophical pondering and political expression.

Heaven Has No Favorites (*Der Himmel kennt keine Günstlinge*)

At first glance there does not seem to be any connection between *The Black Obelisk* and Remarque's next novel, *Heaven Has No Favorites* (1961). One is a largely autobiographical look back at the German inflation year 1923, and the other is a novel about a race car driver and his affair with a tuberculosis patient which takes place some time after World War II. Yet the main theme and the impetus of the story line of *Heaven Has No Favorites* quickly reveals that both novels are related in several ways. The aging race car driver Clerfayt visits his former codriver, Hollmann, at the tuberculosis sanatorium Bella Vista located high in the Swiss Alps. There he meets an attractive and sensitive woman, Lillian Dunkerque, also a patient, who, after learning that her condition has worsened in spite of her diligently following all the hospital's rules, decides to leave the sanatorium and her lover, the Russian emigré Boris Volkov, to live life to the fullest before she dies. She goes to Paris with Clerfayt, and during the trip the two become lovers. In Paris she settles in a small hotel, and to the dismay of her uncle Gaston, a spendthrift who administers her small inheritance, she orders a number of expensive dresses from the fashion house Balenciaga. In the meantime Clerfayt, in Rome on business, meets his old lover, the sophisticated Lydia Morelli, intending to forget his affair with Lillian Dunkerque. Back in Paris, however, he falls in love with Lillian, and later tells her that he wants to marry her, retire from car racing, and take over his company's car franchise which will soon become available in Toulouse. Eventually he takes her to a neglected house on the Riviera which he bought a long time ago, and makes plans for them to live there. But an average, bourgeois life is not what Lillian wants. She decides to leave Clerfayt, but ironically Clerfayt is killed in an unimportant race through the streets of Monte Carlo. At the railway station she meets her former lover, Boris Volkov, who has been looking for her. Lillian goes back with him to the sanatorium, where she dies six weeks later.

The impetus for the novel is Remarque's own enthusiasm for racing and sports cars. When he was working for *Echo Continental* he spent a great number of hours test driving cars equipped with Continental tires in all sorts of weather conditions and terrain. His personal friendship with Rudolf Caracciola, the German racing car champion whom he greatly admired, began in the 1920s and continued until Caracciola's death in 1959. Remarque adds further autobiographical flavor to the novel by having Clerfayt and Lillian drive through the Ticino Canton to Ascona, Porto Ronco, and Lake Maggiore. Clerfayt tells Lillian that he lived in Ascona for a year, and he takes her to some of Remarque's favorite restaurants.

There were also several literary forerunners to *Heaven Has No Favorites*. First was a prose sketch, "Das Rennen Vanderveldes" (Vandervelde's Race) in 1924. Second was a short story entitled "Beyond," which Remarque wrote in the early 1940s and sold to United Artists. In 1947 it was made into a movie called *The Other Love,* in which Barbara Stanwyck (not Marlene Dietrich, as originally intended by Remarque) starred as an American pianist named Karen Duncan who was a tuberculosis patient in a sanatorium romantically set in the Swiss Alps. There she had a relationship with her physician, Dr. Anthony Stanton (David Niven), which was temporarily interrupted by her disenchantment with him. Like Lillian Dunkerque, she left the sanatorium, although she was still ill, trying to live life to the fullest as long as possible, and she became involved with Paul Clermont, a Monte Carlo playboy played by Richard Conte. But Dr. Stanton managed to find her, declared his love for her, and persuaded her to return to the sanatorium with him. Before she died, the two were married. In writing *Heaven Has No Favorites,* Karen Duncan became Lillian Dunkerque, Anthony Stanton became Boris Volkov, and Clerfayt was modeled after Paul Clermont.

During his tenure as editor of the Berlin-based sports and society journal, *Sport im Bild,* Remarque wrote a novel, "Station am Horizont" (Station on the Horizon), which was serialized in 1927/28 in *Sport im Bild* but never published in book form. The hero of the novel is a young nobleman named Kai, who upon visiting Monte Carlo, where he profits from gambling, is persuaded by his friends to drive races in a newly constructed automobile in which he ultimately becomes a winner over his American competitor Murphy. Murphy, however, is his rival not only on the race circuit but also for an attractive American girl, Maud Philby. In the course of the novel Kai gives up the innocent homespun girl of his youth, Barbara, and has an affair with the capricious and attractive Lilian Dunkerque on her yacht. He also manages to win the flirtatious Maud Philby away from his friend Liéven and his competitor Murphy. The novel's romantic elements tend to be forced, as it belabors the issues and strategies of flirtation, as well as the end-of-life philosophies of the aging Princess Parma. It describes the life of dandies on the Riviera and car races at Monza and in Sicily. Remarque emphasizes the technicalities of the races and the psychological entanglements of the novel's playboy characters.

In *Heaven Has No Favorites* Remarque combined the plot of the film *The Other Love* with the racing elements of "Station on the Horizon." In the opinion of most critics it is a novel deeply rooted in the 1920s and reworked from old material. To a Marxist critic like Alfred Antkowiak the novel documents the fact that Remarque has relinquished the achievements of his antifascist novels.[4] For Christine R. Barker and R. W. Last, "it is true that a charge of superficiality would on this occasion be difficult to refute,"[5] but for American critics such as Harley U. Taylor, Jr., *Heaven Has No Favorites* is simply "vintage Remarque."[6] The German press scolded the author for not having written another *Magic Mountain.* The American book reviewers simultaneously lauded him for his skill as a writer and reprove him for his tendency toward sentimentality and philosophical platitudes.

What links this novel to *The Black Obelisk* is Remarque's concern about the meaning of life. He has preserved all the trimmings from his romantic tales about race car drivers and love triangles, but he has created something new: a novel in which the plot elements of car racing and living an intense life to the fullest only serve to explore the questions of life and death. The hero and heroine of *Heaven Has No Favorites* both undergo a significant development in the course of the novel, just as Ludwig Bodmer in *The Black Obelisk*. It is this greater insight into the nature of life and death that is important to Remarque. He is not concerned with the cliché action and its taste for cheap melodrama, a remnant from the Hollywood movie *The Other Love*.

In contrast to "Station am Horizont," it soon emerges that the race driver is not the center of attention. Lillian Dunkerque is the heroine. Since her tuberculosis has become worse, the most reasonable thing for her to do would be to stay in the sanatorium and try to improve her condition by strictly obeying her doctor's instructions. At this point, however, the antirational element of Remarque's vitalistic philosophy comes through: Life cannot be understood by reason, and its problems cannot be solved by reasonable behavior, because, as we see in *The Black Obelisk*, one's actions are not determined by reason alone: "The meager rationality of human beings was there to show them that they could not live by reason alone. People lived by feelings—and being right was no help as far as feelings went" (HF 20). All rational planning in life seems pointless, considering nobody can escape death in the end:

"Nobody escapes," he [Clerfayt] said at last, impatiently. "And nobody knows when and how it will catch up with him. What's the use of haggling over time? What is a long life, anyhow? A long past. And the future always extends only to the next breath. Or to the next race. Beyond that, we know nothing" (HF 31).

It is this philosophy that attracts Lillian to Clerfayt. They seem akin in that they both directly face death; she knows that she will die within a year, and he faces death every time he climbs into his race car. Neither time itself nor the moment of his death seems to mean anything to him. He seems to be living life to the fullest without any regard for the future, and that is what Lillian tries to do during the short time she still has left. It is Clerfayt who, when asked by Lillian what he would do in a situation like hers, replies: "To make one last effort to seize hold of everything that means life, without considering time" (HF 61). Remarque thus underlines the similarities of Lillian and Clerfayt's thinking. For Remarque, choosing the time of death becomes an almost heroic act, something that distinguishes man from animal: "What had Clerfayt once said? That the most desirable thing in life was to be able to choose your own death, because then death could not kill you like a rat or extinguish you, suffocate you, when you were not ready. She was ready. She trembled, but she was ready'' (HF 88). So Lillian sets out to experience life again, life in all its banality. She wants to experience and understand the masses that walk in the streets of Paris, to buy expensive dresses, eat and drink at fashionable places, eat oysters and mussels sold by the street vendors, and drink wine and champagne: "Her whole being was filled with the will to live. To live her own life" (HF 119). Remarque makes it clear that he is not concerned merely with her romantic involvement with Clerfayt, but only insofar as it is part of the theme of living life to the fullest: "She was not out to capture a man; she was out to capture life" (HF 127). When Lillian visits Saint-Chapelle, with its high stained-glass windows flooded with light, she has an almost religious experience that affirms all immortal aspects of her being:

> [The rays] seemed to irradiate the mysterious force that made her heart beat and the blood pulse. It was life itself, and while she sat there, tranquil, without stirring, letting the light rain down upon her and into her, she belonged to it and was one with it. She was not isolated and solitary. Rather, the light received her and sheltered her, and she had the mystic feeling that she could never die as long as it held her so, and that something in her would never die—that part which belonged to this magical light. It was a great consolation, and she pledged herself never to forget it. Her life, those days that still remained to her, she felt, must be like this, a beehive filled with the ethereal honey of radiance: light without shadow, life without regret, combustion without ashes (HF 134).[7]

The epiphanic vision she experiences here in the church thus marks an important stage in her self-realization, and its memory constitutes the undercurrent in her subsequent experience of life around her. In a very mystical sense she intuitively grasps the essential lifeforce within her. This force is indeed present, and Lillian's spiritual change is not unnoticed by Clerfayt. He realizes that she has come into her own, and he feels even more attracted to her. He understands that she

> seeks life like an obsessed huntress pursuing the white stag and the fabled unicorn, hunts it so passionately that the passion is contagious. She has no inhibitions, does not look to either side, and while I myself feel alternately old and used up or young as a child in her presence, there suddenly rise up for me out of forgotten years faces, desires, shadows of dreams, and, above all, like a flash of lightning in the twilight, the long-lost sense of the uniqueness of life (HF 161).

Clerfayt thus has an idea of Lillian's search, although he is not quite able to share it. It is interesting that Remarque adds a mythical dimension to the spiritual and religious experience described in the Saint-Chapelle episode.

However, Lillian reaches an even higher state in her self-realization and in the development of her consciousness. When she watches Clerfayt finish the race after being injured in an accident, the difference between him and herself becomes clear to her: "That fool, she thought, that child who has never grown up! Thoughtlessness isn't courage. He'll crash again. What do they know about death, all these healthy fools? Up in the mountains, they know, they who have had to fight for every breath like a reward" (HF 185). She becomes conscious of how she stands apart from all the superficial people around her. She is able to "see the bare scaffolding" behind the gay and gilded set of a play:

> It was not disenchantment, only a moment of intense clarity of vision. She could not turn back. She knew it now. There was no help to be had from outside. But there was one compensation; the last fountain that remained to her would leap all the higher. Her strength would no longer have to be distributed among a dozen springs, but would be confined to a single one, to herself, and with it alone she had to try to reach the clouds and God. She would never reach them—but was not the attempt already fulfillment, and the falling back of the dancing waters upon themselves already a symbol? Upon herself, she thought. How far you fled and how high you had to aim, to attain that (HF 186).

In this passage Remarque uses language that is almost identical to that of Bodmer in *The Black Obelisk* when he talks to Isabelle when she comprehends the unity behind all being and speaks of attempting the romantic impossible. Lillian's spiritual vision, her insight, is also in the Romantic tradition. Romanticism is indeed "the dissolution of the Veil of Maja, the curtain of deception and confusion over the real world."[8]

Clerfayt cannot follow her in her pursuit; he merely catches a glimpse of what she stands for, and confuses her love for him with his own need for permanence in an ultimately bourgeois setting. He forgets that she can only realize life within a limited period of time. He forgets that, in Lillian's opinion, car races are shallow and superficial and unnecessarily toy with life and death. She considers racing "terribly immoral" and feels that one should not tempt God "out of frivolity" (HF 188). He does not realize that Lillian is slowly detaching herself from him, and that during his last race she has already decided to leave him because he is not what she thought he was. He is a tragic lover in that he thinks about conventional love and emotional commitment at a time when she has become conscious of the fact that there is no future for them.

When she is recovering from a hemorrhage in Venice, Lillian realizes that "if you escaped death frequently, you were reborn just as frequently, and each time with deeper gratitude—so long as you dropped the idea of having a claim to life" (HF 201). Not exactly a profound insight, it nevertheless sets Lillian (and Remarque) apart from Clerfayt. Lillian has given up "the illusion that we have a claim upon life—and with that the illusion that life has been unjust and hasn't granted our claims" (HF 203). Clerfayt still wants to plan his (and her) life and shape the future. The futility of such planning becomes clear when Clerfayt ironically dies before Lillian. According to Lillian/Remarque, there is some kind of compensation in life, because there is no escape: "No one escaped, neither the sick nor the healthy; and that made for a paradoxical compensation" (HF 309). Clerfayt's untimely death has stopped Lillian from rebelling against her disease. However, she does not escape death either; she returns to the sanatorium and dies there.

It is interesting that the language Remarque uses to report her death is very similar to the language he used to describe the death of Paul Bäumer in *All Quiet on the Western Front:*

She died six weeks later, on a bright summer afternoon so still that the landscape seemed to be holding its breath. She died quickly and surprisingly and alone. . . . Her face was distorted; she had suffocated during a hemorrhage, and her hands were close to her throat; but a short while afterwards her features smoothed and her face became more beautiful than Boris had seen it in a long time. He believed that she had been happy, insofar as any human being can ever be called happy (HF 302).

The continuous philosophizing about life and death in the novel is mirrored in the conversations that Lillian has with the young poet Gérard. Gérard is a pure theoretician who likes to talk about and write poetry about death, but runs away when confronted with the reality of death. He runs away when he sees a woman who has died in the street. It comes out in Lillian's relation to her uncle Gaston, who stingily holds on to his money and does not realize that he is getting old. Lillian's conversations with Clerfayt's homosexual friend Levalli in Sicily and with the refined Vicomte de Peystre in Venice and Paris add further dimensions to this constant philosophizing about life and death. For Lillian, the Vicomte "embodied the other side of existence. He had sublimated the anxiety of life into a cult of esthetic cynicism and tried to convert dangerous mountain paths into park ways" (HF 249). In her eyes that is a futile attempt.

By reducing the importance of racing to a metaphor for the senseless quest for life and an expression of arrogant toying with life and death, Remarque has gone far beyond writing a superficial romantic novel. In contrast to his earlier work he has shifted the main theme to the inner development of the two protagonists, Lillian and Clerfayt, the development of his own spiritual philosophy of life and death. Thus, Remarque has developed quite considerably as a novelist since his earlier work.

NOTES

1. Translated from the interpretive essay by Tilman Westphalen in the following German edition: *Der schwarze Obelisk. Geschichte einer verspäteten Jugend.* (Cologne: Kiepenheuer and Witsch, 1989) 393.

2. Injustices similar to those in this epilogue are pointed out by Remarque in the only political article he ever wrote: "Be Vigilant!"(London) *Daily Express* Apr. 30, 1956. There are also obvious parallels to the unpublished essay "Practical Educational Work in Germany After the War," which Remarque probably wrote in Sept./Oct. 1944 for the American Office of Strategic Services. See Lothar Schwindt, "Geheimdienstarbeit: Remarques Schrift *Practical Educational work in Germany after the War,*" *Erich Maria Remarque, 1898–1970,* ed. Tilman Westphalen (Bramsche: Rasch, 1988) 65–78.

3. *Der schwarze Obelisk;* not in the American edition.

4. Alfred Antkowiak, *Erich Maria Remarque* (Berlin: Volk und Wissen, 1980) 143.

5. Christiane R. Barker and R. W. Last, *Erich Maria Remarque* (London, Oswald Wolff, 1979) 95.

6. Harley U. Taylor, Jr., *Erich Maria Remarque* (New York: Peter Lang, 1989) 229.

7. Richard Arthur Firda has given the best interpretation of Lillian's change, although I do not quite see his point in drawing art and its aesthetic appreciation into the discussion. (*Erich Maria Remarque* [New York: Peter Lang, 1988] 235ff.).

8. Firda 238.

CHAPTER SIX

Exile as an Existential Problem

The Night in Lisbon (Die Nacht von Lissabon)

The Night in Lisbon (1961) is perhaps Remarque's most misunderstood novel. Critics have charged that it contains nothing but a rehash of motifs from his earlier novels about exile. But this is true only as far as the basic plot is concerned. In reality Remarque has applied the same technique here as in *Heaven Has No Favorites;* namely, using old motifs to treat a more philosophical theme. This theme was recognized by very few American reviewers; most of them praised the novel for its general aesthetic merits in vaguely positive terms. However, the novel quickly climbed to the top of the American best-seller list.

The story takes place in 1942 in the Portuguese capital, Lisbon. The first-person narrator is staring at a ship anchored in the river Tagus, ready for departure to America on the following day. The narrator has been in Lisbon with his wife for one week. He is a refugee from Hitler Germany who has traveled the same road as so many exiles: first to Paris and then across the Pyrenees to Portugal. He does not have an American visa, and he has just six dollars left in his pocket. At this moment a stranger walks up to him and offers him two free tickets on the ship and a passport with a valid visa in exchange for keeping him company that night and listening to his story. The stranger introduces himself as Josef Schwarz and explains that it is not his real name but the name entered on his passport. His wife is dead and is lying in a coffin in a hotel room.

Josef Schwarz begins to tell his story, beginning in 1938 when, after five years as a refugee from Nazi Germany, he received a still valid passport in the name of an Austrian refugee named Schwarz who died in Paris. The new Schwarz had left his wife, Helen, behind in Germany, believing that they would soon be divorced. He had been denounced by his brother-in-law Georg Jürgens, an *Obersturmbannführer* in the Gestapo, and consequently spent some time in a concentration camp. In the summer of 1939, months before the outbreak of World War II, he used his passport in order to look up his wife in his hometown of Osnabrück in Germany. Much to his surprise, she decided to leave Germany with him and share an exiled life together. Georg and other representatives of Hitler Germany who were trying to persuade Helen to return to Germany followed Schwarz and his wife first to Switzerland and then to France. One week after the outbreak of World War II on September 1, 1939, Schwarz and Helen were arrested and sent to separate French internment camps. After escaping from his camp Schwarz found Helen and fled with her to Bordeaux. In Biarritz Helen collapsed, and Schwarz found out that she was dying from cancer. Through a young American they met in Marseilles, Schwarz and his wife received an American visa; but when Schwarz tried to pick it up at the American consulate, he was arrested and later tortured by the German Gestapo, including Georg. Schwarz finally promised Georg to persuade his wife to return to Germany with her brother. However, on the way to the hotel, Schwarz killed him. He and Helen took Georg's car and fled to Lisbon, where Helen committed suicide by taking poison.

When Schwarz finishes telling his story, he exchanges passports with the novel's narrator. Schwarz has decided to join the French Foreign Legion. The narrator and his wife, Ruth, go to America, but half a year later they are divorced. Ruth marries the young American who obtained Schwarz's visa. The narrator's attempts to find traces of Schwarz in his native Osnabrück prove unsuccessful.

For the first time Remarque has written a novel in which his own native town, Osnabrück, appears under its real name. The streets also have the same names as real Osnabrück streets. For example, Schwarz sees Lotterstraβe with its precise and accurate location mentioned in a newspaper.

There are many other aspects that this novel has in common with earlier Remarque works. Although *The Night in Lisbon* is largely devoted to Josef Schwarz's story, it resembles *Flotsam* in that it reports the fate of two individuals, one of whom manages to escape to America in the end. Moreover, the heroes of the two novels, Josef Schwarz and Josef Steiner, have the same first name. Both men risk their lives and return to Germany in order to see the wives they had left behind. Both Steiner's wife and Schwarz's wife suffer from cancer. In both cases their illness is not revealed until later in the novel.

> In each case the wife had refused to divorce her husband, although in the case of *Die Nacht von Lissabon,* Helen's refusal was more to spite her Nazi brother than out of love for Schwarz. . . . In both novels the return to Germany involves not only a reunion with a loved wife but also an act of vengeance. . . . In *Die Nacht von Lissabon,* the enemy is Helen's Nazi brother, and here the actual details of the avenging murder more

closely resemble Ravic's murder of Haake in *Arch of Triumph,* since both murder victims are lured into a car and then killed.[1]

The importance of possessing a passport, a work permit, and ultimately a visa to enter the United States is another fact common to the other emigré novels. Similarly, the mechanics of crossing the Franco-Swiss border, being sent back and forth across the border, and being jailed, are repeated here. Like Ravic in *Arch of Triumph,* Schwarz and Helen are arrested in France and sent to an internment camp during the first months after the beginning of the war. Schwarz is also tortured by the man he kills, and his motivation for the killing is the same as Ravic's: "It wasn't just revenge—to destroy him would be to save dozens of unknown victims" (NL 130).

The philosophical undercurrents are also similar to those found in other Remarque novels. Schwarz's question: "Does a city stop existing because you've left it? Wouldn't it still be inside you even if it were destroyed?" (NL 110) is reminiscent of similar discussions Bodmer has with Isabelle in *The Black Obelisk.* However, this novel most closely resembles the situation of the characters in *Heaven Has No Favorites.* One might say that the background is different, but the situation is the same. This demonstrates that *The Night in Lisbon* is not so much a novel about exile as it is about a great love. For example, the narrator comments: "It was also the life of a man who loved, or, if that appeals to you, of a kind of saint" (NL 239). In the German text the word *saint* clearly refers to the woman, Helen.

Although there are many similarities, there are also differences. In contrast to *Heaven Has No Favorites,* there is a basic misunderstanding between Helen and Schwarz from the very beginning: when Schwarz comes back to Osnabrück, he has not come to ask his wife to join him in exile, as she wants to believe. The reason for his return is rather "a quiet, stark desperation. My reserves had been used up; my naked instinct of self-preservation had not been strong enough to endure the chill of loneliness any longer. I had not been able to build up a new life" (NL 58). But he dares not tell that to his wife, so in the end he lies and tells her that he had come for her (" 'I came to get you,' I said, 'Don't you know that yet?' " [NL 86]). Helen, on the other hand, does not tell her husband that she is incurably ill. It is not until she collapses for the first time in Biarritz that Schwarz finds out about her cancer. The reader, particularly if familiar with Remarque's other novels, picks up the hints all along, and so does the narrator of the novel, but Schwarz is strangely ignorant of this fact. Both partners in marriage thus hide their quiet desperation from each other. Furthermore, Helen does not follow her husband into exile because she loves him so much. She admits that she has been unfaithful to him, and she continues having affairs during their exile. She follows him because she wants to defy her family, particularly her brother Georg, and leave the humdrum world of a protected bourgeois life in Nazi Germany. Yet the knowledge of her imminent death does make the short time left the more precious to her. Schwarz, on the other hand, is even less conscious of Helen's physical or psychological condition than Clerfayt was of Lillian's, because he does not know that she is ill. Just as Clerfayt makes plans for the future as a car dealer in Toulouse, Schwarz makes plans to escape with Helen to the United States, to live there happily ever after. But whereas Clerfayt knows that Lillian does not have much longer to live, Schwarz does not know for a long time that Helen is going to die soon. Helen realizes the futility of Schwarz's attempts to start a new life, and she commits suicide. The exact reasons for her suicide are not given. We can only guess that perhaps she wanted to end her suffering before it became unbearable or that she did not want to become a burden to Schwarz.

The lack of knowledge regarding Helen's motivations can be accounted for by the fact that, in contrast to *Heaven Has No Favorites*, *The Night in Lisbon* is told from first-person perspectives. There is no omniscient narrator so we learn only what Schwarz himself experienced and thought. Furthermore, in contrast to all other Remarque novels, *The Night in Lisbon* has a narrative framework: the novel's first narrator in many ways only serves as a sounding board for Schwarz. On the other hand, this frame allows the narrator to comment on the story. He is repeatedly asked by Schwarz for his opinion, and he thus "functions as Remarque's own objective commentator on the events and episodes described in the narrator's fateful tale. The listener establishes an aesthetic distance for the reader in a novel whose central plot and framework-story are inextricably interwoven."[2] Schwarz's story is repeatedly interrupted by the narrator's nervousness. He is eager to get to the end because his own concern is not Schwarz and his story, but to get the tickets and visas, fetch his wife, and get on the boat. Like Schwarz before his wife committed suicide, he is an exile who desperately wants to escape and begin a new life in America. This ambition proves ultimately futile. He does achieve his goal of reaching America with his wife, "but the lovers' passport did not bring us luck: Ruth divorced me six months later" (NL 243). Past and present are interwoven as Remarque repeatedly returns to the present situation of Schwarz and his listener. References are continuously made to the restaurant and brothel in which the narrator is listening to Schwarz's story as well as to the presence of German and British guests.

The establishment of a narrative framework places Remarque's novel in the tradition of novella narration dating back to Boccaccio's *Decameron* as well as to many Romantic and late-nineteenth-century German novellas. This novel can perhaps be compared with the stories of *The Thousand and One Nights*, where the continuation of the narrative supposedly prevents the narrator's death. This comparison is supported by the fact that *The Night in Lisbon* also begins with a fairytale motif: a desperate man is offered a lifesaving passport which gives him a new identity for what seems to be a trifle—merely to listen to someone tell the story of his life. This "miracle" is compounded by other such miracles—as when, for example, Schwarz is able to return to Nazi Germany and get his wife out of the hornets' nest. The passport almost works like a magic cloak in this case. When he waves his passport and walks out of the French internment camp, it almost seems as if he were protected by superhuman forces.

However, what distinguishes this novel from all of the other Remarque novels is its shift in emphasis from the usual themes of exile—survival in the emigré situation, a great love in the face of extreme danger, *carpe diem* in the face of having only a short time left to live—to the theme of the overwhelming importance of the motivation for the narration. Of primary importance here is the motivation for the narration rather than its content: Schwarz's basic premise is that "our memory falsifies things to help us survive. It glosses over the unbearable parts of the past" (NL 77). He is afraid that by forgetting part of the past it will be falsified in his mind. The reality of the past is not a reality in and of itself, but exists only in his memory. The failure of his memory results in a loss of the past. Therefore, he must make the past concrete by telling it to someone so that he will not forget it himself. In this way, the reality of the past is more lasting. Only on this premise can the large reward the listener receives, the passport and the ticket for the passage to America, be justified. The only reason for Schwarz's flight was the possibility of a new life with his wife in America. Now that she has passed away, his flight to America has become pointless. He must now first concentrate on preserving the memory of his life with her and his love for her, including everything she has done for him as well as her unfaithfulness. Once recalled and narrated, memories become fixed in the mind of the listener, and they can no longer change:

> A miracle is never perfect when it happens; there are always little disappointments. But once it's gone for good and nothing can change it, mem-

ory could make it perfect and then it would never change. If I can just call it to life now, won't it always stay the same? Won't it stay with me as long as I live? (NL 108).

Somewhat later Schwarz questions the existence of reality vis-à-vis the memory of the reality:

"Who are we?" he said. "Who are you? Who am I? And what about all those people and those who are gone? Which is real, a man or his reflection in the mirror? A living human being or his memory, his image shorn of grief? Have my dead wife and I become a single person? . . . Is she completely mine now that she exists only as a phosphorescent shimmer under my skull, now that she can answer only when I want her to and as I want her to? Or, after losing her once, am I losing her for a second time, a little more each moments as her memory pales? . . . I've got to hold her, don't you see that?"(NL 108–09).

The reason why Schwarz must speak is to save his memory from himself. The listener does not analyze Schwarz's logic; such an analysis would reveal the paradox of memory: this reality is equally subject to falsification through the listener's mind, particularly since Schwarz's fate does not directly concern him. However, Schwarz does not think in these terms; the listener is more objective, in his opinion. Therefore, he is better able to preserve an objective memory of what he is told: "You'll keep it safe," Schwarz tells him; "with you there's no danger. Your memory won't try to wipe it away to save you, as mine does to save me. With me it's in bad hands; even now, that last rigid face is crowding out the others like a cancer" (NL 135–36).

At the end of the novel, however, we find out that the preservation of Helen's memory is not the only thing that concerned Schwarz. He also wants to be consoled, and to be assured that in spite of her unfaithfulness to him, Helen loved him. In the final analysis, what Schwarz was really searching for was a means of coping with the loss of his wife; to come to terms with their relationship and to find his own identity again. In order to describe this process Remarque skillfully uses the themes of Nazi Germany and exile as a backdrop. Rather than writing an exciting novel about the dangers and adventures of life as an emigré—a historical novel—Remarque has written a psychological novel that deals with the question of the reality of an individual's experiences and various means of preserving these experiences through narration.[3]

Yet one could go one step further and argue that, for Remarque, even this narration cannot accomplish what it undertakes. There is no way of holding on to anything from the past, neither a memory nor human being. Human beings cannot possess each other; they deceive and lie to each other in spite of their love. The narrator's existential viewpoint at the end supports this reading: "Why all this talk about degrees of possession, when the illusory word 'possess' means merely to embrace the air?" (NL 243).

Shadows in Paradise (Schatten im Paradies)

Remarque's last novel, *Shadows in Paradise*, was published post-humously in 1971 in Germany. The American edition appeared in 1972. According to Remarque's American agent, Felix Guggenheim, Remarque had continued revising the novel until his death on September 25, 1970.[4] In spite of this, there are a number of unresolved inconsistencies in the book. For example, the hero could not possibly have experienced all the narrated events prior to his arrival in America. Because of this fact, it is safe to assume that Remarque had not finished revising his novel. The publisher should perhaps have edited the manuscript more carefully. Critics also generally agree that the novel is not one of Remarque's best,[5] but it is nevertheless of considerable importance, not only because it documents Remarque's later political views, but also because in it Remarque deals with America for the first time.

In some respects the novel continues where *The Night in Lisbon* had left off: Robert Ross, a former journalist, was in a German concentration camp, but he was ultimately released because he was not Jewish. Ross fled Germany and spent several years in hiding in an art museum in Brussels; at night, when no one was around, he was able to leave his hiding place and become intimately familiar with the collections. Later, in Paris, he aided an art dealer with phony antiques and paintings before being interned by the French at the beginning of World War II. In the general confusion of the capitulation he fled France and, equipped with a forged passport, traveled on a freighter to the United States.

He is given the address of a Russian immigrant, Melikov, who works at the Hotel Reuben, a seedy hotel off Broadway in New York, where Ross stays. His integration into American life seems to be going very well. He manages to quickly acquire a rudimentary knowledge of English and because of his knowledge of art, particularly Chinese bronzes, he soon finds a job at an antique shop. Later he works as a salesman with Silvers, an art dealer who sells French impressionist paintings from his home. He is a guest at the homes of several other German emigrés, mostly Jews, including the successful Vriesländer and the homesick Betty Stein, who provides a spiritual home for many immigrants until she dies from cancer. He meets Harry Kahn, who courageously saved many people from the German Gestapo but later commits suicide in America. Ross has an affair with the attractive Natasha Petrovna, a model of Russian descent, who was born in France. He accompanies Silvers on a trip to Hollywood, where he is employed by a movie director as an adviser for anti-German propaganda films. When the war is over, he decides to go back to Germany. He soon realizes that in Germany he can no longer fit in. In retrospect, his affair with Natasha seems to have been the most important experience of his life.

There are a number of autobiographical details of interest in *Shadows in Paradise*. Robert Ross is a thinly veiled Erich Maria Remarque. Like Remarque, Ross is a former Catholic who was disillusioned because the Church concluded a concordat with Hitler's Germany. The apartment on 57th Street where Natasha temporarily resides clearly resembles Remarque's New York apartment. The New York restaurants Ross frequents with Natasha—for example, the El Morocco—were among Remarque's favorite restaurants. Ross's preference for New York over Hollywood parallels Remarque. The Beverly Hills Hotel where Silvers lives and the Garden of Allah where Ross stays Remarque knew from his own stays in Los Angeles (he usually stayed at the Beverly Hills Hotel). Remarque rented a house in Westwood similar to the house he describes in which the beautiful but incredibly stupid Carmen lives. Ross's activities as an antique shop employee and a salesman for an art dealer give Remarque the opportunity to demonstrate his expertise in the fields of Chinese bronzes and French impressionist paintings. Ross's initial detention on Ellis Island upon his arrival in New York is reminiscent of Remarque's former wife Jeanne's detention. Several of the minor characters are modeled after historical figures: the writer Moller, who commits suicide by hanging himself from a chandelier in his room, is modeled after the leftist expressionist writer Ernst Toller, who also hanged himself in his New York hotel room; the writer Hasteneck, who also commits suicide, is a reference to the writer Walter Hasenclever, who committed suicide in Aix-en-Provence; and Betty Stein immortalizes a certain Betty Stern, who operated a kind of salon that was frequented by artists and writers in Berlin during the Weimar Republic. There are other direct references to the writers Thomas and Heinrich Mann, Lion Feuchtwanger, and Stefan Zweig—all German exiles from Nazi Germany.

Remarque was quite familiar with America and with the situation of the German exiles in America. As this novel takes place in the United States, he seizes the opportunity to voice his opinion on the New World. Unfortunately, his point of view does not yield many insights, but enumerates the usual clichés. Only superficial observations typical of European visitors are made. For example, American coffee is bad for the European taste; it is strange that you can eat meals in a drugstore; America is obsessed with youthful appearance and slender figures, and most American women are perpetually on a diet ("The women here eat like rabbits while whole continents starve" [SP 273]). There are no prostitutes, but almost everyone sees a psychiatrist. Many middle-aged women are described as looking ridiculous with their heavy makeup and their hats like swallows' nests on their heads, obviously a commentary on the fashion of the 1940s.

New York is much more to Ross's liking than Los Angeles, which clearly reflects Remarque's own preference. New York seems more honest. It is indeed quite different from European cities, but beautiful in its own right. Looking out the window of an apartment on the eighteenth floor of a Park Avenue building, Ross describes what he sees:

> Down below lay New York in the summer heat, like an African city with skyscrapers. One could see at a glance that this city of steel had not grown slowly and organically, taking on the patina of centuries, but had been built quickly and heedlessly by determined men unencumbered by traditions. And because their aim had been not beauty but efficiency, they had created a new and daring beauty that was neither classical nor romantic (SP 110).

In contrast to New York, Hollywood gives Ross even more of "a strange sense of unreality, that though the country was at war one saw no sign of it. Here in Hollywood the war was a purely literary conception" (SP 204). In Hollywood members of the SS are just movie extras and war has been reduced to a game. Hollywood is full of swindlers and members of sects; it is a city where the sale of the soul to the devil has become reality. As a European, Ross has the feeling that in Hollywood he lives in a vacuum, somewhere between Japan and Europe. Consequently, he discovers his love for New York.

Through Silvers, the art dealer, and his newly rich customers Remarque satirizes the business practices of American art dealers he was very familiar with through his own art collecting. Remarque's satire extends to the American business world in general. He refers to new millionaires who acquire art solely in order to raise their social prestige; the refined French impressionist paintings represent a sharp contrast to their own unrefined tastes. Ross's "financial education by Silvers is an example of Remarque's criticism of America's predilection to materialize culture and make consumers out of art patrons."[6] Remarque portrays the glittering film world of Hollywood, where money and position give people the kind of self-confidence that does not need confirmation through art. Consequently, the sly art dealer Silvers is surprisingly unsuccessful in this city.

However, in his later works Remarque was interested in commenting not only on his American environment, but also on Germany and its guilt with respect to the rise and success of the Nazis. Thus, the novel repeatedly echoes his views as previously expressed in *Spark of Life* and *The Black Obelisk*. According to Remarque, the Germans' main flaw is that they like to take orders. By taking orders they feel released from individual responsibility for their actions. Remarque expresses his belief that the Nazis were not just a small group within the German populace; the majority of Germans were Nazis. To him all Germans are Nazis because they knew about the crimes and atrocities that were committed at the time in Germany and they did nothing about it. The German generals are criminals who ordered their soldiers to keep fighting long after it was clear that the war was lost. In addition, he assumes that after the war many Germans would not remember anything that had happened.[7] At the end of the novel Ross returns to Europe and feels just as alienated there as in America:

> It was a return to a strange country, a return to indifference, cowardice, and concealed hatred. No one remembered having belonged to the party. No one accepted responsibility for what he had done. I wasn't the only one with a false name. Hundreds had changed passports and gone scot-free—a new generation of murderers. The occupation authorities were well-intentioned, but there was little they could do; they depended for their information on Germans who either feared retaliation or whose code of honor forbade them to "soil their own nest." . . . Many had no recollection that concentration camps had ever existed. I came up against silence, against walls of fear and indifference" (NT 304).

Thus, even late in his life Remarque continued to accuse Germany for not adequately dealing with its Third Reich past. The guilty were not being prosecuted, and the people had not learned from their experience.

Remarque has also continued the theme of exile in *Shadows in Paradise*. Several characters from earlier novels reappear here. Dr. Ravic now practices medicine in New York. The hotel where Ross stays is similar to Ravic's hotel in Paris, and his affair with Natasha is in many respects similar to Ravic's affair with Joan. Ross's past experience has a lot in common with that of Ravic and of Schwarz in *The Night in Lisbon*. However, there is one significant difference between *Shadows in Paradise* and the earlier novels about exile. The earlier novels took place in Germany of other European countries where the refugees were either exposed to life-threatening experiences, or where they were imprisoned, interned, sent to other countries, sought after, handed over to the Gestapo, and so on. In America the refugees either have been given a permanent resident visa or reside and work illegally in a vast and free country which, in spite of its involvement in World War II, is extremely liberal and generous in its treatment of emigrés. After all, America is a country where immigrants live far removed from the European war scene. It is a country ready and willing to integrate those who have come to seek refuge on its shores. Remarque tries to compensate for the lack of life-threatening situations in his novel by repeatedly referring to Ross's former life in a German concentration camp, his life in Paris and in hiding in the Brussels art museum. Remarque also introduces other characters such as the courageous Kahn, who has gone through much hardship and danger to survive and fight against the Nazi regime. Remarque uses these stories as a contrast to life in the United States, where the war is hardly noticed. The only indication that a war is being waged is the increased presence of military uniforms. The war is so unreal in America that it merely serves as a pretext for Hollywood propaganda movies.

The main theme of the novel is thus not the dangers under which the refugees from Nazi Germany live, but their more or less successful attempts to find a new life in America. Kahn reiterates the situation of the exiles in the United States most clearly. For him the emigrés' lives have no significance because they are unable to participate in the fight against Hitler Germany. They are simply onlookers, and that is the reason for their "so shadowy and almost obscene" existence (SP 180). Ross himself later recalls his life in America:

> I went back into the shadowy existence, as if I were living on a magical island in a storm, which, however, had only two dimensions and not three. It was different from the years in Europe where the third dimension consisted of the fight against bureaucracy, government offices, gendarmes, the fight for residence permits, illegal work, with customs officers and with policemen, with the struggle for the naked existence."[8]

Remarque uses a number of very different characters in order to demonstrate various means of coping or not coping with the new environment, although he clearly focuses on the German-Jewish middle-class refugee community in New York. The financially most successful refugee is Vriesländer, a Jew who invested a considerable part of his fortune in the United States before the export of capital became illegal in Germany— that is, even before the Nazis' rise to power. Vriesländer is obviously very successful on the American stock market, and his attempts to become an American seem somewhat forced in the novel. His naturalization is celebrated as he changes his name to Daniel Warwick. Only English is spoken at his home, and only American wines and liquor produced in America are served. On the other hand, he scrupulously seeks business opportunities in Germany after the war, and he correctly predicts the phenomenal economic rise of the new West Germany. Vriesländer has thus totally broken with his German-Jewish past. He lives only in the present and tries to assimilate himself and his family (through his daughter marrying a "real" American) to his new environment. Modest professional success is also demonstrated by such characters as Tannenbaum, an actor who now plays SS officers in Hollywood's anti-Nazi films.

In contrast Remarque presents such characters as Moller, the writer who is unable to publish anything in the United States; the typically German writer Frank, whose books do not sell; the adventurer Kahn, who is famous for daredevil feats in dealing with the German Gestapo but who cannot accept that all the future holds for him in America is being a radio salesman and eating icecream. He is not accustomed to the safety in which he now lives and cannot find any meaning to his new life. "Enthusiasm over life," he says to Ross, "is like champagne. Once the cork is drawn, it goes stale" (SP 199). In the character of Betty Stein, who is like a mother to many emigrés, Remarque has painted a picture of a Jewish woman who cannot accept that Germany has changed and who continues to live in the Berlin of the Weimar Republic. She refuses to understand that the Berlin she once knew has crumbled in the air raids. She eagerly awaits her return to Berlin after the war and consequently gives up in her fight against cancer when the Germans' last military offensive seems to be temporarily successful. Living in the past, she embodies the exact opposite to Vriesländer, the practical man of the present. Ross tries to exist somewhere between the two extremes represented by Vriesländer and Betty Stein, but he cannot make the final decision to live in America. He still has too many unresolved questions about his past in Germany to allow him to start afresh.

It is not until the end of the war, when the emigrants are confronted with the choice of whether or not to return to a destroyed Germany, that more serious problems arise. Kahn forces Ross to realize that the most difficult part of their gypsy existence will not come until they face the question whether they belong anywhere any more. The emigrés live in the illusion that all their problems will be solved by the end of the war and do not understand that the end of the war is really the beginning of a new journey.[9] It will be "a terrible letdown for us refugees," Kahn says to Ross. "Up to now we have been sustained by the thought of the injustice that was done to us. And now all of a sudden the injustice is gone. We'll be able to go back. What for? Where? And who wants us? How *can* we go back?" (SP 267–68). The emigrés' romantic nostalgia and the hatred they lived by have proven false, for one cannot hate what has been destroyed. It seems that through the words Kahn speaks, Remarque is describing his own situation, his ability or inability to return to Germany. Since Remarque did not return to his native country, but to Switzerland instead, he accepted the practical consequences of this debate in *Shadows in Paradise*. Thus the novel is a reflection of Remarque's own suffering and uprooted feeling as an exile in America, in spite of the luxury he enjoyed.

Keeping Remarque's previous novel with its hero, Schwarz, in mind, one might expect that the hero in this novel, Robert Ross, would also undergo some kind of inner development. However, this is the case only in a very limited sense. Ross has unjustly suffered at the hands of the Nazis. We never learn what exactly happened, but he has much in common with Koller from *Spark of Life,* except that he was accidentally released and managed to escape to America. Like Koller, Ross was a journalist, and worked in the crematorium of the concentration camp, where he witnessed people being hung from gambrels. Like many of the characters in the other exile novels Ross seeks revenge, particularly against one of his torturers whom he is unable to find after his return to Germany. At the end of the novel he has given up in his search for revenge and searches now for a feeling of fulfillment of justice:

> Those who had been tortured and murdered and burned could not be brought back to life. But there was something that could be done, and I was going to do it. The source of my determination was not revenge, though it sprang from the same primitive roots; it was the feeling that crime must not go unpunished, for if it did the foundation of morality would collapse and chaos would reign" (SP 298).

Taking revenge and fighting for justice are significant only insofar as they prevent Ross from integrating into life in America. He does have new experiences in America. He has the feeling of being part of normal life again; he gets a job, makes money, and has a love affair. He realizes that he is again living in a society with concerns and worries different from that of a refugee. When he comes home in the evening to Natasha's apartment, he experiences what it is like to come home and have someone waiting for you. Still, he has doubts about this new sense of security. His longing for love is fulfilled in Natasha, but Natasha and he repeatedly assure each other that their relationship is only temporary and they need each other only to heal their respective inner wounds. It is not until his return to Europe that Ross realizes Natasha was more than a pastime and the fulfillment of a longing for warmth and love. In the final analysis Ross is a hero who had a chance and was emotionally unable to make use of it. He realizes that he now lives in a new environment, but is unable to adapt to it. He wants to avenge those injustices done to him and others but realizes that he cannot. Thus, he does not develop and does not gain substantial new insights. The novel fittingly concludes with a very vague statement which, through its sentimental tone, merely masks the lack of development and insight: "One can never go back; nothing and no one is ever the same. All that remained was an occasional evening of sadness that we all feel because everything passes and because man is the only animal who knows it" (SP 305).

This insight is not exactly earth-shattering, and demonstrates the lack of action and a clear message of *Shadows in Paradise*. Perhaps Remarque has merely projected his own existence as an exile in the United States onto his hero Robert Ross, whose circumstances in exile were so different from his own. One could thus conclude that the novel is as autobiographical as *All Quiet on the Western Front, Three Comrades,* or *The Black Obelisk*. However, this autobiographical background unfortunately results in an unrealistic portrayal of a refugee in the character of Robert Ross, and merely projects

> a romanticized inner image of his own inner self. Autobiographical sentimentalism blurred his view and consequently led him to write an unconvincing story. The narrative powers he displayed when he wrote about the haunted existence of the refugees in his other novels were impaired by personal sentimentalism when dealing with his own life. And so *Shadows in Paradise* suffers from the incongruity of Remarque's own successful life in exile and the struggles of his fictional refugee hero.[10]

Shadows in Paradise did capture a spot on the German best-seller list—perhaps as the result of an enormous advertising campaign. The American reviews were almost uniformly devastating. They criticized the novel for a lack of action and a questionable hero who does not really know what he is after in life. Only several minor characters found grace in the eyes of the critics.

NOTES

1. Christine R. Barker and R. W. Last, *Erich Maria Remarque* (London: Oswald Wolff, 1979) 117–18.

2. Richard Arthur Firda, *Erich Maria Remarque* (New York, Peter Lang, 1988) 248.

3. Firda (254) writes: "Political evil and cultural barbarism are only a background against which men stand out as victors or losers in the struggle between common and extraordinary suffering."

4. Firda 261.

5. E.g., Barker and Last 143.

6. Firda 265.

7. Most of these statements are not contained in the American edition of *Shadows in Paradise*.

8. Translated from the German edition, p. 244; not in the American edition.

9. See p. 306 of the German edition; not in the American edition.

10. See Hans Wagener, "Erich Maria Remarque: Shadows in Paradise," *Exile: The Writer's Experience,* ed. John M. Spalek and Robert F. Bell (Chapel Hill: University of North Carolina Press, 1982) 247–57.

CHAPTER SEVEN

Trying His Hand at Drama

The Last Station (Die letzte Station)

In his novels Remarque proved himself a master of written dialogue. In addition, his novels distinguish themselves by their episodic structure. Every couple of pages a particular scene ends, often culminating in a witty or unexpected solution or a general truth. It was thus relatively easy to convert his novels into movie scripts, or to adapt them for dramatic presentation.[1] When once asked to what he contributed his successes, Remarque replied: "Perhaps to the fact that I am a kind of a playwright manqué; that is, a direct writer, not a detour writer. All my books are written like dramas. One scene follows the other. The author as *deus ex machina* has been eliminated. He appears neither as a commentator, nor as an omniscient contact man."[2] From this observation one would expect that Remarque would have also excelled in the field of drama. However, he did not.

Apart from earlier attempts at drama, the manuscripts of which have not survived, his first successful project as a dramatist goes back to his work for the film industry. In 1954 Remarque wrote a film story for the Austrian film, *Der letzte Akt (The Last Ten Days)*, directed by G. W. Pabst. Unfortunately, his contribution to the script was unclear, as the film's final credits read: "According to a film story by Erich Maria Remarque. Scenario by Fritz Habeck." Thus, it would appear that Remarque produced a film treatment which was then transformed into a drama by a collaborator who wrote the screenplay. In the story he continued the analysis of fascism which he had initiated with *A Time to Love and a Time to Die*. *The Last Ten Days* was a film about the nervous breakdown and suicide of Adolf Hitler (played by Albin Skoda) in the bunker beneath the Berlin Chancellery during the Russian invasion. The scenario was based on the 1950 book *Ten Days to Die* by Michael A. Musmanno, the American judge of the International Tribunal at the Nuremberg Trials, where between 1946 and 1948 upper-echelon Nazis and high-ranking German officers were tried and sentenced for their war crimes. The film followed the actual historical action very closely, except for the introduction of the fictional character Wurst (played by Oscar Werner), "a young captain who is finally shot in a confrontation with

Hitler himself. Wurst's idealism is sensitively contrasted with Hitler's decision to flood the Berlin subway system as a last stand of insanity against the Allied invasion of Berlin."[3] During an interview in Vienna, Remarque stated that he had taken on the project as a result of his lifelong concern with fascism in postwar Germany. As we have seen in the novels of the time, this was Remarque's fundamental concern during the mid-1950's. His only published political essay, "Be Vigilant!" written for the London *Daily Express*, employed the last words uttered in the film as its title.[4] This essay expressed his concern about Germany's failure to confront its Third Reich past and the resurfacing of neo-Nazism in West Germany.

The play *Die letzte Station* (The Last Station), somewhat of a spinoff of *The Last Ten Days*, premiered on September 20, 1956, at the West Berlin Renaissance Theater as part of the celebrated *Berliner Festwochen*, a cultural festival. For the premier performance the title was changed to *Berlin, 1945*. It is unfortunate that the drama has never appeared in print. There remain, therefore, several differing versions, all adaptions for stage presentation.[5]

The action of the drama takes place on April 30 and May 1, 1945, in a room on the west side of Berlin. During an air raid two concentration camp prisoners manage to flee from a square where the SS has already begun shooting prisoners in light of the approaching Russian troops. One of the two prisoners, Ross, has been given the address of a man named Wilke, who can provide sanctuary. When he gets to Wilke's apartment, he learns from a woman, Anna Walter, that Wilke does not live there any more, having been arrested four years ago by the Gestapo. Ross cannot venture into the street again; the SS are after him. All he has to wear is prisoner's striped pants, and he has no papers. He persuades Anna to hide him until dark. She gives him her husband's uniform, hides his tattooed concentration camp number on his arm with a bandage, and presents him to her neighbor Grete as her cousin Peter Vollmer. When *Oberscharführer* Schmidt searches the premises with two other SS men, Anna explains that Ross had lost his papers while drunk, and that he spent the previous night with her. When the second escaped prisoner, the Jewish Professor Koch, is brought in, he does not betray Ross. Instead, to escape further torture he jumps out of the window to his death. At this point the radio announces that Hitler is dead and the Russians are entering the city. Concerned for their own safety, the SS leave the apartment without arresting Ross. Ross stays overnight with Anna.

The next morning many people display white flags, sheets, and towels from their windows to indicate surrender. Anna tells Ross that her husband, to whom she had entrusted information about Wilke's anti-Nazi activities, betrayed him to the Gestapo, in order to save his own skin. After Ross has left the room to prevent the block warden Körner from denouncing him Schmidt enters, now wearing civilian clothes. He is carrying the identity papers of a murdered concentration camp inmate which are supposed to protect him when the Russians arrive. He tries to blackmail Anna to hide him for a while. When Ross returns, Schmidt threatens to kill him. By a clever ruse Anna manages to force Schmidt to drop his gun. At gun-point, Ross forces Schmidt to climb onto the window sill, promising to kill him just like he killed Ross's prison mate. Suddenly the Russians arrive. Ross and Anna toss the guns out of the window.

At this point Schmidt is protected by his false identity papers; Ross has no papers, but he is wearing the uniform of a German officer. In the ensuing interrogation Schmidt successfully incriminates Anna and Ross, but the Russians do not have time for lengthy investigations. To extract the truth, they tell Schmidt and Ross to line up against the wall and prepare for execution. Schmidt loses his self-control and tries to bribe the Russians. In an effort to escape he is shot and killed. Ross is then taken to the Russian command post, but he is soon able to return to Anna. Together they will have a new beginning.

The play was fairly successful in Berlin; it was not produced on other German stages. Years later the task of creating an English adaptation was entrusted to the American playwright Peter Stone. Stone's adaptation was called *Full Circle*.[6] It was first performed under this title in 1973 in Washington DC, and in the same year in New York City. Produced and directed by Otto Preminger, it featured Leonard Nimoy as Ross (now called Rohde) and Swedish actress Bibi Andersson as Anna. In *Full Circle* Anna is Wilke's widow. At the end, the Russian captain tries to force the former journalist Rohde to work for the new communist Germany. When Rohde refuses to trade one form of dictatorship for another and thus to compromise his principles, he is taken away by the Russians to receive some "guidance" at an "information center."

To the readers of Remarque's novels *The Last Station* does not present anything new. To begin with, in *The Last Station*, Ross bears the same name as the hero of *Shadows in Paradise*, who has also been a concentration camp inmate. Steiner, in *Flotsam*, jumps out of the window to escape torture by the Gestapo—although in this case he takes his former torturer with him to his death. The combination of a life-threatening situation and a love story is obviously vintage Remarque. The theme of denunciation typifying the Third Reich has already been treated in *A Time to Love and a*

Time to Die. The idea that the Nazis would retreat underground and then resurface has already been expressed by Schmidt in the epilogue of *Spark of Life*. Furthermore, the theme of the final revolt of the individual against the dehumanizing dictatorship of the Third Reich has already been explored in all the novels that deal with the Third Reich, whether directly or indirectly. Finally, Remarque's anticommunism—his belief that communism, like fascism, is a dictatorship—has already been illustrated in *Spark of Life*.

Remarque depicts Ross's rapid development from a man who at the outset is haunted by the SS to a person who, finding hope, rebels and fights against his enemy and who ultimately succeeds in regaining his freedom and the love of a woman. *The Last Station* is full of action, and the language vacillates between street slang and expressions of lyrical softness. The adherence to the classical unity of time, place, and action, and the localization of the plot in a history-making point in time, impart to the play a compactness and urgency;—although, unfortunately, the action can hardly be deemed realistic. Each situation seems artificially constructed: the right things happen at the right time; for example, the Russians have the good sense to make the correct decision. Finally, the concentration of familiar, almost cliché motifs considerably diminishes the literary value of the play.

"The Homecoming of Enoch J. Jones" ("Die Heimkehr des Enoch J. Jones")

The discovery of the manuscript of a second play among the Remarque papers housed in the Fales Library of New York University was made in 1986. It is still not yet available in print. The Erich Maria Remarque-Archiv/Forschungsstelle Krieg and Literatur of the University of Osnabrück successfully persuaded Remarque's widow, Paulette Goddard, to consent to a limited number of performances (twelve), to be given only by nonprofessional actors and only on a noncommercial basis. On October 15, 1988, roughly thirty years after it was written, the drama was first performed by the Osnabrück *probebühne*. Some inconsistencies in the manuscript, revealing its yet-unfinished state, had to be ironed out before the performance.

As with *Shadows in Paradise*, "The Homecoming of Enoch J. Jones" takes place in the United States. The scene of the action is a small American town; the time is July 1956. Enoch J. Jones, believed missing in action in the Korean War and assumed dead, was in reality taken prisoner. Now, five years later, he is coming home. A red carpet is unrolled. Local newspaper and television reporters and the minister and mayor are anxious to welcome him. But nothing remains the way he left it. His wife, Lolly, whom he married just two months before being drafted, has married his war buddy and friend, William Smith. Newspaper and television hounds are fighting for the rights to his war experiences. The mayor and the local pastor are primarily concerned with using the publicity of the "hero" who has come home. The army, represented by Major Ickles, accompanies Jones back home with military honors.

Remarque has invented this situation in order to satirize the American consumer society of the mid-50's. The political issues he brings to the stage are the Cold War, the anticommunism of the McCarthy era, the fear of an atomic war, and the inherent dangers of the American rearmament of West Germany. The fate of the individual is satirically set against the background of the sociopolitical situation.

Jones is an honest man whose war experiences have served to enlighten him. The naive ideals he clung to during the war and during his time as a POW have all been betrayed. His experiences have left him averse to militarism and hollow patriotic phrases; he is repulsed by the grandiose military reception extended to him, perceiving patriotism as a purely hypocritical veil for self-interest. It seems that the only person who truly understands him is his Czech house servant, Liese Ravic. An emigré and former guerrilla fighter, she is equally repelled by the kind of reception Jones receives. Jones and Ravic are drawn to each other even more when the others try to protect the appearance of idyllic harmony. They leave together.

Although the action takes place in America, Remarque does not aim his satire solely at the United States; it may easily be construed as being directed toward West Germany. In criticizing the American values of the 50s, he hopes to alert Germany to the dangers of importing the American way of life and attitudes. The concurrent rearmament and bifurcation of Germany suggest parallels to the political situation in Korea. Such parallels are unconsciously manifested throughout the entire play. In order to intensify the reference to Germany, the stage decor of the debut performance was set in a style of Germany in the 1950s.

Familiar Remarque themes, such as exile, abound. Statements and ideas are reiterated to excess, and the play suffers from emotionalism, sentimentalism, and a fibrous thread of pathos; it is clearly outdated by today's standards. Such defects are, of course, easily exonerated, since the play is after all unfinished. Nevertheless, such affective tendencies figure regularly in Remarque's work.

NOTES

1. As late as 1984 scenes from his novels relating to Osnabrück were performed in that city under the title *The Black Obelisk*.

2. "Interview mit sich selbst (XVII): Erich Maria Remarque. Größere und kleinere Ironien meines Lebens" ("Interview with Himself. Greater and Smaller Ironies of My Life") *Die Welt,* Mar. 31, 1966.

3. Richard Arthur Firda, *Erich Maria Remarque* (New York: Peter Lang, 1988) 288.

4. Remarque, "Be Vigilant!" *Daily Express,* Apr. 30, 1956.

5. The following plot summary refers to the original play. This version leaves out the final scene with the Russians.

6. Peter Stone, *Full Circle: A Play by Erich Maria Remarque* (New York: Harcourt, Brace, 1974).

CHAPTER EIGHT

Fame Through Hollywood

Remarque's fame in the United States, and to a certain extent in Europe, was prompted not only by his novels but also by the films that were adapted from the novels. In addition, the sale of the film rights to Hollywood giants provided him with a considerable source of income. Seven of Remarque's novels were transformed for the screen, with *All Quiet on the Western Front* and *Arch of Triumph* appearing in one film version and one television version each. The episodic structure and the prominence of dialogue in his novels render the adaptation to film relatively easy. In addition to these stylistic qualities, all his books are not only action-packed but also feature a love story, almost a "must" for the Hollywood movies of the 40s and 50s. It is therefore safe to assume that, with the exception of his first novels, the notion of having his work turned into movies may have profoundly influenced Remarque in his choice of style in the first place.

Soon after the publication of *All Quiet on the Western Front,* Carl Laemmle, the German-born president of Universal Pictures in Hollywood, acquired the movie rights. He even journeyed to Germany in order to strike a deal with the author himself. The film was produced by Laemmle's son, Carl Laemmle, Jr., and directed by Lewis Milestone. Maxwell Anderson, coauthor of the stage play *What Price Glory,* and George Abbot, coauthor of *Broadway,* collaborated on the screenplay adaptation. The young Lew Ayres was selected for the role of Paul Bäumer. World War I was re-created on the 930-acre Irvine Ranch in Southern California. A large military camp was constructed and twenty acres of land were dynamited to simulate an authentic-looking No-Man's Land; two thousand soldier extras were hired, and to imbibe the spirit of the story they lived by military regulations for the duration of the filming. The reenacted battles used over twenty thousand pounds of black powder, and tons of dynamite. Six thousand land mines were planted and detonated. As part of a bombardment scene a French village spanning ten acres was built and then destroyed; a canal was dug for the scenes in which Paul and his friends were visiting the French girls. Finally, a 280-ton crane was employed so that the camera could be positioned as close as possible to the action.

Released in 1930, the film was a great international success. Lewis Milestone and Lew Ayres became celebrities overnight; Milestone received an Oscar for direction. Additional Oscars were awarded for the writing. Since it was one of the first sound films, *All Quiet on the Western Front* was also noteworthy in film history.

But the showing of the film in Berlin was controversial: on December 5, 1930, in the Mozartsaal Theater on Nollendorf-Platz, with hundreds of viewers in attendance, Goebbels (who later became Hitler's propaganda minister) made a surprise appearance. Affronted by the film he had white mice released and stink bombs placed in the auditorium. Panic reigned among the moviegoers, and police had to be called in to clear the theater. The remaining performances for the evening had to be canceled. A nationwide uproar resulted. Goebbels decried the film as an American assault on German nationalism. The public controversy precipitated the banning of the film several weeks later "for reasons of maintenance of safety and public order."

In 1939 the film was reissued in the United States. A pictorial prologue was added, and a narrator interrupted the film approximately a dozen times, effecting anti-German overtones. In 1952 the film was shown again in Germany; a completely reconstructed version of the original, which included all scenes that had been cut, was produced by the Zweites Deutsches Fernsehen, a government-sponsored German television station, in 1984.

Another book Universal Studios acquired the screen rights to was *The Road Back*. This novel was so similar to *All Quiet on the Western Front* that the film was not released until mid-summer 1937. The movie was a commercial success, although (or maybe because) it did not adhere very closely to the novel. As Harley U. Taylor, Jr., writes: "Although John King [Ernst] and his supporting cast gave credible performances, the movie was flawed by an unfortunate tendency to slapstick humor not found in Remarque's story. This tendency had actually begun with the semi-comedic portrayal of Tjaden by 'Slim' Summerville in 'All Quiet.' The humor became more heavy-handed in 'The Road Back' with the increased emphasis on comedy for Tjaden and the casting of Andy Devine in the role of Willy. With Andy Devine in the part, Remarque's rough-and-ready, bluff Willy inevitably deteriorated into a near buffoon."[1]

The film of Remarque's next book, *Three Comrades,* was produced by Metro-Goldwyn-Mayer. Joseph Mankiewicz was the producer, and Frank Borzage the director. None other than F. Scott Fitzgerald was hired to write the screenplay. Robert Taylor starred as Robby Lohkamp; Margaret Sullivan portrayed Patricia Hollmann; Franchot Tone played Otto Köster, Robert Young was cast as Gottfried Lenz. Problems arose when Fitzgerald became unwilling to stick to the plot of the novel. Displeased, Mankiewicz commissioned Ted Paramore to collaborate with Fitzgerald who took great umbrage at this intrusion. Mankiewicz was obliged to step in, rewriting a number of the scenes.

Unfortunately, before the film was released, Louis B. Mayer decided to preview it for a representative of the German consulate in Los Angeles. Being disenchanted with the portrayal of Nazi violence, the German official "suggested" to Mayer that communists be substituted for Nazis, and threatened a boycott of all MGM feature films in Germany. Mayer was amenable to the request, but Mankiewicz refused. Released in June, 1938, the film enjoyed considerable commercial as well as critical success, although the sentimentality underlying Remarque's novel was even more pronounced in the movie. Instead of representing the quiet despair of three friends in the aftermath of World War I and their enthusiasm about cars and car racing, the film concentrated on Lohkamp's love affair with Pat Hollmann. One redeeming feature: Margaret Sullivan was nominated for an Academy Award.

The film that was based on *Flotsam* was entitled *So Ends Our Night*. It was released by United Artists and produced by David L. Loew and Albert Lewin. Frederick March starred as Josef Steiner. Completed in November 1940, several months before the book was published, the film "was warmly received by theatre audiences, but critical reviews were mixed. . . . It was generally conceded that the cast was good but that more could have been done with the story."[2]

The film version of *Flotsam* contained one central deviation from the plot of the novel. In the film version Kern's imminent deportation by French authorities is thwarted when Ruth Holland declares her intention to marry her employer, a French university professor. In order to circumvent a family scandal should one of its members marry a Jewess, the professor arranges the acquisition of American papers for both Ruth and Kern. "The film's ending, however, seriously misrepresents Remarque's major point of view that, first, Mexico's offer to open up its doors to large [numbers of] German exiles and expatriates was a humanitarian gesture, and, second, that countries like France and Switzerland were prepared to turn away refugees who failed the rigid tests of citizenship requirements."[3] *So Ends Our Night* ends with Ruth and Kern preparing to go to America. We can only suspect that the American film industry wanted this new ending to preserve the myth of America as a nation that opens its gates to the oppressed and persecuted of the world.

The filming of *Arch of Triumph* brought unexpected problems. It was produced by Enterprise Pictures and released by United Artists in 1948. Charles Boyer was cast in the role of Ravic, and Ingrid Bergman in that of Joan. Both had worked well together in the 1944 filming of *Gaslight,* and were good choices for *Arch of Triumph.* But Louis Calhern failed to capture the complexities of the character Boris Morosow and Charles Laughton was unconvincing as the sadistic Gestapo officer Haake. Many other characters were simply omitted—for example, Kate Hegstroem. In spite of its seemingly superior casting, the movie was not a commercial success. It failed to capture the spirit of the novel, and often deviated from the original story line. For instance, Ravic was depicted as an Austrian, and the romantic love story eclipsed the story of the haunted exile. In addition, "film critics were not given a rounded characterization of Joan and did not accept the credibility of her relationship with Ravic. . . . It is apparent that for a number of reasons, the literary impressionistic style of *Arch* resisted screen adaptation."[4] Critics further claimed that the movie focused exclusively on a melodramatic love story, and that the exile background and atmosphere of Paris on the eve of the outbreak of World War II had not been convincingly and realistically rendered. The movie lost approximately $2,000,000, and in 1949 Remarque sued Enterprise Studios for breach of contract in order to collect his $50,000 for the movie rights.

The filming of *A Time to Love and a Time to Die* was not completed until 1958. Shooting began in August 1957, in Berlin. Remarque himself allegedly participated in the writing, but apparently did not contribute enough to be included in the credits. More obvious was his contribution as an actor: he himself played the teacher Pohlmann. He rather enjoyed the acting and, according to the film critics, did a credible job impersonating the teacher who, in both the novel and the film, served as spokesman for his personal humanitarian ideas. The shooting was done in the ruins in the Tiergarten area of Berlin, and the Russian battlefront scenes were shot in northern Bavaria.

Director Douglas Sirk focused his film on the tragic love of a German soldier and a young girl, relegating the polemic of the German Nazi state and the theme of collective guilt and national responsibility to the background—an interpretation he deemed more appropriate for the American film audiences of 1957. He assumed that film audiences were sufficiently knowledgeable about recent German history to eliminate the necessity for further elaboration. Thus he created a film about a love that knew but an ephemeral state of happiness, doomed by the destructive circumstances during which it flowered. His point of view was certainly congruent with Remarque's way of thinking.

Although this film lacks the intensity of *All Quiet on the Western Front* to even warrant a comparison with it, in many reviews it suffered from such a comparison. It was well made and is particularly interesting because of Remarque's own (and only) appearance as an actor. The reviews were more positive in America than in Germany, where the same brand of criticism was voiced as about the book: like Remarque, Sirk did not have wartime experience in Germany.

Heaven Has No Favorites was produced for the screen in 1977. Entitled *Bobby Deerfield,* it was produced and directed by Sydney Pollack for Columbia Pictures/Warner Brothers. Filming took place on location in Europe—LeMans, Paris, Lake Como, Florence, Leukerbad in the Swiss Alps. Unfortunately those scenes in the novel that take place in the Ascona, Lake Maggiore, and Porto Ronco area (Remarque's home), where Clerfayt took Lillian in the novel, were not included in the film. Clerfayt, played by Al Pacino, appears as an American Grand Prix driver named Bobby Deerfield; Lillian appears under her original name, Lillian Dunkerque, played by Marthe Keller. The skeletal plot of the novel was preserved, but the personality of the characters was altered: "Deerfield is a far more brooding, introspective character than Clerfayt who, by comparison, seems less problematic and far more likable. Much of this is a result of Al Pacino's grim and wooden interpretation of the character. Marthe Keller is more skillful in capturing some of the essence of Lillian but almost entirely lacks her vulnerability."[5] The entire thrust of the novel was redirected. It is Bobby Deerfield who, through his relationship with Lillian, undergoes a fundamental inner transformation; he is able to come to terms with his own past, becoming "more open and vulnerable to emotions and human relationships. Pollack's film, more than Remarque's novel, suggests that it is Deerfield who has lost the balance between work and personal life. The death of Deerfield's lover, Lillian, however, restores this equilibrium and signals the rebirth of Deerfield himself."[6]

Neither *The Night in Lisbon* nor *Shadows in Paradise* was made into a film but after Remarque's death there were three more television productions of his novels. The first one, in 1979, was a new American production of *All Quiet on the Western Front,* directed by Delbert Mann. Richard Thomas played Paul Bäumer, and Ernest Borgnine portrayed Katczinsky.

The war scenes were shot in Czechoslovakia, with units of the Czech army serving as extras. A town which could be destroyed was also available: the small town of Most, close to the German border, had already been designated for relocation, as a result of the discovery of a rich coal seam underlying its foundations. The new film version was just as faithful to the book as the 1930 version had been. Only the ending was substantially different: in the 1930 version Paul Bäumer was killed by a sniper's bullet as he was reaching out for a butterfly resting on a sandbag—undoubtedly the most poignant scene of the movie. Since this scene did not appear in the novel, and since the television company of the 1979 version had acquired the film rights to the novel only, because of copyright laws it was not permissible that Paul Bäumer die in the same manner as in the old film version. A meadow lark was therefore substituted for the more poetic butterfly.

A television version of *Arch of Triumph* with Maximilian Schell and Suzanne Pleshette in 1980 was a failure. Only a few days after shooting began, it had to be broken off for lack of funds. A new attempt began in March 1984 with a different set of producers and a new cast of actors. Ravic was now played by Anthony Hopkins, and Joan Madou by Lesley-Anne Down. The film was shown on May 29, 1985, as the CBS Wednesday Night Movie. Although Anthony Hopkins's interpretation of Ravic made the character appear somewhat more taciturn and less outgoing than in the novel, and although many of the capricious aspects of Joan Madou's character were not developed, the performances of both actors were very credible. Moreover, the film adhered very closely to the novel. Finally, the atmosphere of Paris shortly before the outbreak of the war was rendered with great precision, especially the accuracy of the costumes.

It was not until 1988 that *The Black Obelisk* was made into a television movie for the Zweites Deutsches Fernsehen. The director was Peter Deutsch, the script was written by Gerd Angermann. Udo Schenk portrayed Ludwig Bodmer, Rainer Hunold played Georg Kroll, and Karina Theyenthal appeared as Geneviève.

NOTES

1. Harley U. Taylor, Jr., *Erich Maria Remarque* (New York: Peter Lang, 1989) 91. Most of the facts reported in this chapter are taken from Taylor's book.
2. Taylor 151.
3. Richard Arthur Firda, *Erich Maria Remarque* (New York: Peter Lang, 1988) 122.
4. Taylor 137–38.
5. Taylor 238.
6. Taylor 245.

CONCLUSION: A FINAL ASSESSMENT

When Erich Maria Remarque embarked on his writing career, he sought in vain to forge a style of his own; imitating the style and motifs of his literary milieu, the contemporary literary *Jugendstil (l'art nouveau)*, he composed contrived poetry and a novel, *The Dream Room*, which was rife with clichés and charged with pathos and artificial passion. His next novel, *Station on the Horizon*, published in serial form in *Sport im Bild*, was only a few steps ahead in literary quality. Again, Remarque obviously desired to please his reading public, the readership of a society journal. It is no wonder that neither of these novels has ever been reprinted and that the later Remarque was embarrassed about his first attempts to establish himself as a writer.

It was not until *All Quiet on the Western Front* that he discovered his true voice—a realistic style and a subject matter that departed radically from his previous literary attempts. Although Remarque merely alludes to rather than explicitly asserts his pacifistic convictions, the book was rightfully perceived as an antimilitaristic, antinationalistic, and pacifist statement of the first order, rejecting the convictions of the old generation, faulting them for the war and its deleterious effects on the young people who were forced to fight it. In writing *All Quiet on the Western Front* Remarque had indeed made himself the spokesman for an entire generation, not just of Germans but of all nations who had experienced the horrors of war and did not want the experiences ever to be repeated. *All Quiet on the Western Front* is *the* novel about World War I, and arguably the best war novel of all times. If Remarque had not written any other book, this novel alone would ensure a place for him in the history of world literature.

The criticism of the society that sent its young people into the war is continued in the logical sequel, *The Road Back*. But in spite of its convincing war scenes and psychologically convincing description of the estrangement of the returning soldiers, it soon becomes obvious that this novel is much more artificially constructed than *All Quiet on the Western Front* in that individual characters are "assigned" certain problems of reintegration into a postwar society. In hindsight, *The Road Back* does not have by far the literary quality of *All Quiet on the Western Front*.

The "lost generation" theme that was continued in his second novel was brought to a conclusion in *Three Comrades*. This book may thus be interpreted as the final part of a trilogy. It shows Remarque's abilities declining further as he tries to describe the final loss of comradeship during the Weimar Republic. The elements of sentimentality which in his preceding two novels he had been able to suppress had now gained the upper hand and showed the danger of the author's slipping to the level of magazine literature. *Three Comrades* therefore represents a low point in Remarque's development as a writer.

It had become obvious that Remarque was in dire need of a new theme for his literary endeavors, and he found it in the theme of exile. Although Remarque himself did not experience the hunger, starvation, persecution, internment, or imprisonment as many of his characters, his exile novels were in many respects as realistic as *All Quiet on the Western Front*. He was able to identify with the characters he described and to understand their concerns. He realistically described their haunted existence and the problems they encountered with passports and work permits in countries unwilling to accept them, both in *Flotsam* and in *Arch of Triumph*. In both novels Remarque skillfully combines stories of exile life with sentimental or melodramatic love affairs and heated dialogue in which the partners engage. On the one hand this makes for exciting reading; on the other hand there must be more to a novel to make it an artistic success. Whereas *Flotsam,* therefore, rightfully was not a great success, *Arch of Triumph* became Remarque's second worldwide best-seller. This was not due to its treatment of the theme of exile, but rather because of its demimonde milieu and its theme of murder and love. The novel will probably be remembered as a slick example of entertainment literature of the 1940s.

Shortly after World War II, Remarque embarked on a new theme in his novels and wrote about life inside the Third Reich. Thus, he abandoned his previous custom of writing only about firsthand experiences. His descriptions of German concentration camps in *Spark of Life* and life in a World War II German city in *A Time to Love and a Time to Die,* a city which is being demolished by air raids, were severely criticized. The German reviewers accused him of a lack of firsthand knowledge of his material. It is true that for both novels Remarque thoroughly researched official reports and documents as well as conducting personal interviews with eyewitnesses. But probably neither one of the novels will be considered great literature by literary historians. Whereas the vitalistic theme of the will to survive against all odds in *Spark of Life* is a bit dated and clearly places its author in the first half of the twentieth century, the overriding importance of the love story amidst the destruction of a German city during the Third Reich in *A Time to Love and a Time to Die* prevents the novel from focusing on its more serious agenda: the battle of conscience raging inside its hero. However, in spite of these weaknesses, the development of the heroes of both novels from passive acceptance of their fate as dictated by the political system, through an individual, critical analysis, and finally to active resistance is testimony to Remarque's change into a political writer with a message. They demonstrate once more that, in spite of his own opulent life style, Remarque was taking the side of those who were victims of twentieth-century history and that he was now posing questions that would increase his readers' political awareness.

This message also echoes in *The Black Obelisk*, at least in the epilogue and in many critical asides within the text. The novel is not only a social critique of the inflation year 1923 and its effects on an average German town; it is also an autobiographical, critical self-analysis and a personal existential quest. In contrast to Remarque's earlier novels about himself and the Weimar Republic, its ironic distance and raucous humor and its clear political statement make *The Black Obelisk* far superior to his other novels about the Weimar Republic, *The Road Back* and *Three Comrades.*

The pondering over fundamental existential questions which Remarque began in *The Black Obelisk* is a theme continued in *Heaven Has No Favorites* with its conversations about life and death and about how to persevere in the face of death. Racing and high life on the Riviera and in Paris constitute only the background to the fundamental questions which Remarque addresses by constructing extreme situations. Thus, he again shows that he has developed considerably as a writer and as a human being. Although the high life of the protagonists, the emphasis on racing, and a playboy-type existence at times overshadow the deeper meaning of the book, future criticism will probably recognize the more timeless themes, and the novel's merits.

The shift to existential issues was prominent in these two novels. It is evident again in Remarque's last two novels, *The Night in Lisbon* and *Shadows in Paradise*. Here the exile question is of lesser importance, providing only the pretext for the existential issues. But whereas *The Night in Lisbon* successfully treats a philosophical theme, thus making the book into a modern novel and one of Remarque's best, *Shadows in Paradise* fails to state its problem clearly and does not draw a convincing picture of its main character.

This final evaluation of Remarque's novels clearly demonstrates the author's literary development. Remarque is not only the writer of *All Quiet on the Western Front*, the most widely read war novel ever written, and *Arch of Triumph*, the international best-seller about exile. One may very well argue, that none of his later works attained the stature of *All Quiet on the Western Front* which has become a classic on both sides of the Atlantic. But in several novels which appeared after 1945 Remarque demonstrates a much clearer political consciousness than for example, in those written during the Weimar Republic and the Nazi era. A review of Remarque's entire work demonstrates that its author never deviated from his basic humanist belief of advocating peace and respect for the individual human being.

BIBLIOGRAPHY

Works by Erich Maria Remarque

Die Traumbude: Ein Künstlerroman (The Dream Room). Dresden: Verlag der Schönheit, 1920.

Station am Horizont (Station on the Horizon). *Sport im Bild* 1927: nos. 24–26; 1928: nos. 1–4.

Im Westen nichts Neues. Berlin: Propyläen, 1929. [*All Quiet on the Western Front.* Trans. A. W. Wheen. Boston: Little, Brown, 1929.]

Der Weg zurück. Berlin: Propyläen, 1931. [*The Road Back.* Trans. A. W. Wheen. Boston: Little, Brown, 1931.]

Drei Kameraden. Amsterdam: Querido, 1938. [*Three Comrades.* Trans. A. W. Wheen. Boston: Little, Brown, 1937.]

Liebe deinen Nächsten. Stockholm: Bermann-Fischer, 1941. [*Flotsam.* Trans. Denver Lindley. Boston: Little, Brown, 1941.]

Arc de Triomphe. Zürich: Micha, [1946]. [*Arch of Triumph.* Trans. Walter Sorell & Denver Lindley. New York: Appleton-Century, 1945.]

Der Funke Leben. Cologne: Kiepenheuer and Witsch, 1952. [*Spark of Life.* Trans. James Stern. New York: Appleton, Century, 1952.]

Zeit zu leben und Zeit zu sterben. Cologne: Kiepenheuer and Witsch, 1954. [*A Time to Love and a Time to Die.* Trans. Denver Lindley. New York: Harcourt, Brace, 1954.]

Der schwarze Obelisk: Geschichte einer verspäteten Jugend. Cologne: Kiepenheuer and Witsch, 1956. [*The Black Obelisk.* Trans. Denver Lindley. New York: Harcourt, Brace, 1957.]

Der Himmel kennt keine Günstlinge. Cologne: Kiepenheuer and Witsch, 1961. [*Heaven Has No Favorites.* Trans. Richard & Clara Winston. New York: Harcourt, Brace, 1961.]

Die Nacht von Lissabon. Cologne: Kiepenheuer and Witsch, 1962. [*The Night in Lisbon.* Trans. Ralph Manheim. New York: Harcourt, Brace, 1961.]

Schatten im Paradies. Munich: Droemer, Knaur, 1971. [*Shadows in Paradise.* Trans. Ralph Manheim. New York: Harcourt, Brace, 1972.]

CRITICAL WORKS

BIBLIOGRAPHIES

Erich Maria Remarque. Der Nachlaß in der Fales Library, New York University. Ein Verzeichnis. Ed. Thomas Schneider, Erich Maria Remarque-Archiv/ Forschungsstelle Krieg und Literatur. 3 vols. Osnabrück: Universität Osnabrück, 1989.

Owen, C. R. *Erich Maria Remarque: A Critical Bio-Bibliography.* Amsterdam: Rodopi, 1984.

Westphalen, Tilman et al. *Erich Maria Remarque. Bibliographie. Quellen, Materialien, Dokumente in 2 Bänden* (Bibliography, sources, materials, documents in 2 volumes). Osnabrück: Universität Osnabrück, 1988.

BOOKS

Antkowiak, Alfred. *Erich Maria Remarque: Leben und Werk* (Life and Work). Berlin: Volk und Wissen, 1980. A Marxist interpretation and evaluation of Remarque's works which consequently devalues Remarque's emphasis on the individual and criticizes his heroes' lack of political activity.

Barker, Christine R., and R. W. Last. *Erich Maria Remarque.* London: Oswald Wolff; New York: Barnes and Noble, 1979. A useful and balanced introduction to Remarque in English which includes some anti-Marxist polemics. Weimar Republic novels as well as those dealing with exile are grouped together.

Baumer, Franz. *E. M. Remarque.* Berlin: Colloquium, 1976. A cursory German introduction the Remarque's life and works, mostly based on articles and memoirs by others.

Erich Maria Remarque zum 70. Geburtstag am 22. Juni 1968 (For Erich Maria Remarque on his 70th Birthday on June 22, 1968). Cologne: Kiepenheuer and Witsch; Munich: Kurt Desch, 1968. A *Festschrift* published jointly by two of Remarque's German publishers, without scholarly ambition.

Firda, Richard Arthur. *Erich Maria Remarque: A Thematic Analysis of His Novels.* New York: Peter Lang, 1988. The first part is heavily biographical and does not sufficiently address the topic of its subtitle. However, it contains a good analysis of Remarque's later novels. Many details are incorrect.

Rüter, Hubert. *Remarque. Im Westen nichts Neues: Ein Bestseller der Kriegsliteratur im Kontext* (*All Quiet on the Western Front:* A Best-Seller of War Literature in Context). Paderborn: Schöningh, 1980. The definitive book on *All Quiet.*

Taylor, Harley U., Jr. *Erich Maria Remarque: A Literary and Film Biography.* New York: Peter Lang, 1989. A biography which at times is not far above weekly magazines in style and content. The treatment of the novels rarely goes beyond providing a plot summary. Contains many facts about the movie versions of Remarque's novels.

Westphalen, Tilman, ed. *Erich Maria Remarque: 1898–1970*. Bramsche: Rasch, 1988. A collection of eight scholarly essays on Remarque and his work, as well as a chronology of his life and a bibliography. Includes many photographs of Remarque.

INTERVIEWS

"All Quiet on the Western Front: Why It Was Written. Interview with Erich Maria Remarque." London *Observer* Oct. 10, 1929: 17–18.

Eggebrecht, Axel. "Gespräch mit Remarque." *Die literarische Welt* June 14, 1929.

Gelder, Robert van. "An Interview with Erich Maria Remarque." *Writers and Writing*. New York: Scribner's, 1946. 377–81.

Liepmann, Heinz. "Remarque und die Deutschen." *Zürcher Woche* Nov. 30, 1962. Also in: *Die Welt* Dec. 1, 1962.

ARCHIVES

Most of Remarque's personal papers, manuscripts, and reviews of his works are at the Fales Library, New York University. A microfilm copy of these holdings as well as other primary and secondary material is available at the Erich Maria Remarque-Archiv/Forschungsstelle Krieg und Literatur, Universität Osnabrück.

INDEX